REMARKS ON

PRISONS AND PRISON DISCIPLINE

IN THE UNITED STATES

By DOROTHEA LYNDE DIX

With a New Introduction by

LEONARD D. SAVITZ

Temple University

Reprinted from the Second Edition, 1845

PATTERSON SMITH

Montclair, New Jersey, 1967

REMARKS

ON

PRISONS AND PRISON DISCIPLINE

IN THE

UNITED STATES.

By D. L. DIX.

Second Edition,

FROM THE FIRST BOSTON EDITION.

'I have endeavored to clear my understanding from all prejudices, and to produce a frame of mind fitted for the investigation of truth, and the impartial examination of these great questions.'   LIVINGSTON.

PHILADELPHIA:

JOSEPH KITE & CO., PRINTERS.

1845.

TO THOSE

ENLIGHTENED AND BENEVOLENT MEN

IN THE

UNITED STATES,

WHOSE CONTINUED, AND WELL DIRECTED EFFORTS HAVE PROCURED AN

ALLEVIATION OF THE MISERIES OF PRISONERS, AND WHOLESOME

REFORMS IN PRISON DISCIPLINE,

THE FOLLOWING PAGES ARE RESPECTFULLY INSCRIBED,

BY

D. L. DIX.

It is a commentary of some importance on our times that the phrase "female social reformer" should automatically conjure up an image of an ancient dowager chaining herself to a lamppost, chopping saloon bars into small pieces or engaging in similar foolishness. It strains our sophisticated imagination that any woman, without major psychiatric disturbances, could devote her life to something which, by our standards, is as inconsequential as the reform of penal institutions and insane asylums. Given our present preoccupation with the problem of physical survival, our incredulity is perhaps understandable. Nevertheless, this constitutes one more indication of the enormous shift in our social ethos over the past century. A hundred years ago such ameliorative enterprises were praiseworthy and vigorously applauded, and for no one was the applause louder than for Dorothea L. Dix, who today is completely unknown to our mythical "intelligent layman." Even sadder perhaps is that she has been equally forgotten by the academic and professional criminologist who is notoriously indifferent to (ignorant of, more likely) the history of his chosen discipline, particularly in the area of penology, which is now regarded as of interest only to those with a bent towards the arcane and antiquarian. Dorothea Dix — humanitarian, reformer, and philanthropist, described by her contemporaries as "the most useful and distinguished woman America has yet produced," judged by many as superior in dedication if not accomplishment to Florence Nightingale, closely associated with William Ellery Channing, Horace Mann, Charles Sumner, Francis Lieber, Franklin Pierce — is truly, in the words of her definitive biographer, Helen Marshall, America's "forgotten Samaritan."

Born in Hampden, Maine, in 1802, Dorothea Dix was teaching school by the time she was fourteen years of age and publishing elementary text books by age twenty-two. (Some of her texts were phenomenally successful; *Conversations on Common Things*, for example, went through sixty editions.) She early became a disciple of Channing, whose simple doctrine, "Man must be sacred in man's sight," became the dominating force in her life. After a breakdown in 1834, probably caused by overwork, and the death of her grandmother, which left her financially secure for life, she became aware of and involved with the frightful conditions in the institutions for the insane. In 1841, while teaching Sunday school classes in a Cambridge, Massachusetts, jail, she was shocked to discover that insane persons not accused of crimes were indiscriminately mixed with sane prisoners, and hardened criminals with first offenders. All prisoners were without adequate medical treatment or moral counsel. She soon visited every prison, house of correction, alms-house, and insane asylum in the state as the basis for her first *Memorial to the Legislature of Massachusetts* (1843), which strongly attacked the inhuman conditions she found. After meeting violent reaction, she was firmly supported by Charles Sumner, although her social service activities were to remain contentious for the rest of her life. This was a woman who relentlessly pursued the improvement of conditions for the insane, sick, and imprisoned with enormous energy for over forty years. When she died at the age of eighty-five, she could count 123 asylums and hospitals established largely because of her efforts.

Dorothea Dix's *Remarks on Prisons and Prison Discipline in the United States* is the resumé of her four-year investigation of all the prisons in the New England and Middle Atlantic states. She was manifestly aware of the divergent penal philosophies then being widely debated and the part they played in the intellectual life of her times. Reformation, not social revenge, she believed should be the central element in the prison program. She was, inevitably, incensed by the conditions she discovered at most penitentiaries. Next to prison security, her primary concern was with the prisoners' health, conformity to prison discipline, and instruction ("as the parent instructs the child"). Moral regeneration was her ultimate goal.

At the outset of her report, Miss Dix recognizes the controversy then raging between adherents of the "two great experimental systems": the Auburn system (in which the prisoners work together in silence by day and sleep at night in individual cells) and the Pennsylvania system (in which the prisoners are kept in solitary confinement by day and night). She deplores the denigration of either system on the basis of failures stemming from poor institutional management. Cruelty, injustice, laxity of discipline were prevalent in prisons operating under either system, much of it caused simply by unfit or too frequently rotated prison administrators. She believes that penitentiaries should not be conducted as businesses with the aim of showing a profit, thereby removing in her view one of the chief arguments in favor of the Auburn system.

Miss Dix finds much to criticize in the prisons of her day. She contends there should be no collecting of "admission money," a cruel practice whereby persons could visit the prison to be amused by the curious antics of the inmates. At one point she suggests that the best way to aid the prisoner is to let him learn to work in prison, but later she is convinced that moral suasion is the best means to reformation. She is against rewards in prison for good behavior (so important to later programs based on a "mark" system) because such rewards merely increase disciplinary problems through quarrels and jealousies (an early expression of what in modern terms is referred to as the conflict between the "treatment" and the "custodial" approach). Her natural instincts are against corporal punishment. But even the lash, which she regards as particularly abhorrent, is in her view occasionally necessary in prisons run on the Auburn plan as the only means of reducing the "insurrectionary" spirit of certain inmates. For other prisons she considers the milder punishment of the cold shower-bath to be an effective way of reducing infractious prisoners to compliance. While admitting that the maintenance of discipline is the first problem to be faced in any prison, she concludes that society and the prisoner are best served by providing each inmate with moral instruction and religious teaching. The central role in this program, to which she devotes the largest section of her work, is to be played by the chaplain, who will educate the conscience as well as the intellect.

While Miss Dix is reluctant to formally align herself with either side in the Pennsylvania versus Auburn controversy, her sympathies are clearly with the former. She does not wish to create any new prison society to carry out her philosophy but would work through existing organizations, particularly the Philadelphia Society for Alleviating the Miseries of Public Prisons, which was the Pennsylvania system's chief advocate. She is explicitly against "free association" of prisoners. (Yet, in all honesty, it is difficult to ascribe free association to the Auburn system, since the inmates, though eating and working together, were kept in separate cells at night and were never permitted to talk to one another.) She finds the silent system inferior in almost every regard to the separate system (the latter best exemplified by the Eastern State Penitentiary at Cherry Hill, Pennsylvania). She sees discipline under the Auburn system as more difficult to maintain and more likely to require flogging; the diet is bad; the water is inadequate in amount and quality; and the ventilation and heating equally inferior. (Not all these deficiencies in Auburn-plan prisons, Miss Dix might have noted, are intrinsic to the silent system.)

Miss Dix does not believe the Pennsylvania system is perfect; almost all institutions have prisoners with excessively heavy sentences, and too many prisoners are pardoned, reducing the certainty of punishment. Nevertheless, she cites with complete approval the view of John Haviland that the Pennsylvania system is the most perfect system of prison discipline that the wisdom of man has produced. Her confidence in the separate system as representing the most rational and viable philosophy was further supported by the

1844 report of the Inspectors of the Eastern State Penitentiary, which held that all of the earlier predictions on the success of the separate philosophy had been entirely realized. (Curiously, two years earlier a committee of the New York State Assembly sounded the death knell of the Auburn system by ending their report with the statement that "silence does not reform anyone." As a matter of fact both the Pennsylvania and Auburn philosophies were soon to fade from the American scene.) While she says she will not vindicate nor justify the separate system, it had in her view so many excellences and so few defects that she advocates its universal use in the United States.

Dorothea Dix in many ways is a splendid product of her times. Her life was unswervingly dedicated to correcting injustice in the world. It might be said in retrospect that her philosophy when translated into prison programs was impractical and, indeed, it did contain many contradictory features. Thus, she was interested in reformation but only after discipline and security had been fully attained. She was against the lash, but not under certain conditions. Whipping was bad but the shower-bath punishment was acceptable. Prisoners should work but for no substantial rewards. Sentences were often excessive but the pardoning power should not too frequently be used to correct them. Beyond this it can even be argued from a century's experience with corrections that her programs for inmate instruction and edification are demonstrably ineffectual.

In the final analysis, however, these criticisms are of less importance than the simple fact that she was concerned (in our current parlance, "involved") in a worthy moral enterprise. There is today no comparable individualized interest, let alone dedication, to similar problems. Lacking any systematic philosophy our society is given to a glib acceptance of "treatment" which encompasses such a range of diffused and varied projects, programs and ideas, that the term is for all practical purposes meaningless. The public gives a casual nod to the necessary reform of the criminal but beyond this there is to be found only indifference and a system of punishment which lurches forward inertly, unchanged for decades. We lack any meaningful intelligence about what prison accomplishes, so that a recent attempt to measure the impact of institutional life in California might be considered truly revolutionary. Dorothea Dix's passion, her range of interest, and her dedication are, alas, no longer fashionable.

LEONARD D. SAVITZ
Temple University

September, 1966

REMARKS

ON PRISON DISCIPLINE, &c.

THE difficulty of commanding time, to answer in detail numerous written and verbal inquiries respecting the result of four years personal study and observation of the Penitentiaries, Jails, and Alms-Houses, in the Northern and Middle States, with occasional visits to others adjacent, has induced me to put into this form some remarks illustrating the history and present condition of American prisons.

I owe this to the high standing and intelligence of those who have honored me by the expression of confidence in my judgment and impartiality ; and sincerely regret that I have so little leisure to give to the illustration of these important subjects, upon which volumes might be written, showing the origin, progress, and prospects of a Reform so eminently affecting social order, and the Civil Institutions of our Republic.

Years of unintermitted labor and vigilance are necessary for producing practically beneficial results, through the influences of these disciplinary institutions.

Society, during the last hundred years, has been alternately perplexed and encouraged, respecting the two great questions— how shall the criminal and pauper be disposed of, in order to reduce crime and reform the criminal on the one hand, and, on the other, to diminish pauperism and restore the pauper to useful citizenship ? Though progress has been made, through the efforts of energetic and enlightened persons, directed to the attainment of these ends, all know that society is very far from realizing their accomplishment. We accord earnest and grateful praise to those who have procured the benefits at present possessed ; and with careful zeal, we would endeavour to advance a work, which succeeding generations must toil to perfect and complete.

Moralists and philosophers, with pietists and philanthropists, have urged upon communities the truer course of employing early *preventive* measures, rather than of expending the energies, at a late period, in futile attempts to govern and lead by correct and virtuous habits, the long-time criminal, and the life-long indolent and ignorant.

The great benefactors of individuals and of communities are the enlightened *Educators ;* the wise-teaching, mental and moral instructors and exemplars of our times. These are they who, working effectively and effectually, reduce the crowded cells and apartments of our prisons and our almshouses, and raise impregnable defences against the inroads of idleness and vice, poverty and crime ! Men need knowledge in order to overpower their passions and master their prejudices. ' To see your brother in ignorance,' said Jeremy Taylor, ' is to see him unfurnished to all good works ; and every master is to cause his family to be instructed, every governor to instruct his charge, every man his brother, by *all possible and just provisions. For* if the people die (spiritually) for want of knowledge, those who are set over them shall die for want of charity.'

Equality of knowledge, whether intellectual or moral, and equally clear conceptions of distinctions between right and wrong, cannot be possessed under the most careful instruction ; for the capacity of man is infinitely varied ; his early condition will modify his perceptive powers ; acquisition will depend on many causes, all of which cannot be brought equally into action ; but all men may be taught, who are not deficient in mental capacity,—that is, who are not idiots, or furiously mad,—the observance of those laws and rules which give moral vigor and safety to society. Let the conscience be enlightened ; let accountability and responsibility be demonstrated ; and added to this, let the intelligent, the prosperous, and the elevated in rank, be elevated by justice, uprightness, kindness, and strong integrity,—and the humble, the lowly, *the weak*, of whom there are so many, and who are so sorely tried and tempted, will have powerful aid in maintaining their virtue, in resisting vice, and in forbearing crime.

During the last ten years especially, public attention has very generally been drawn to the two great *experimental* systems, which have come in our country to be designated—we will not here inquire how correctly—the Auburn system and the Pennsylvania system. Of those under the first named form of discipline, the best examples at this time, beyond all question, are that at Auburn in Western New York, the Connecticut prison at Wethersfield, and the Maryland penitentiary at Baltimore. The latter system is excellently illustrated in the Cherry-Hill, or Eastern Penitentiary at Philadelphia, and the Western Penitentiary in Alleghany City, Pennsylvania. Good examples of the ' *silent* system,' applied in county prisons, may be found at Hartford and New Haven in Connecticut, and at South Boston, Massachusetts ; and, of the ' *separate* system,' in Dauphin county at Harrisburg ; at West Chester, in Chester county ; and at the prison in the Moyamensing district, Philadelphia county.

Some writers on the reformed systems of penitentiary government in the United States, have labored to advance a favorite plan by depreciating that to which they have been adverse ; adducing examples of cruelty, personal abuse, and gross mismanagement, throughout every department of the prisons to which they were inimical. This mode of illustrating a system is altogether unfair and unjust. Who does not know that the best system ever devised by human wisdom, if badly administered, may become the fruitful source of almost incredible miseries and corruption, as at one time the prisons at Auburn, Sing Sing, Concord, &c. The good system, ignorantly or viciously administered, becomes as great an evil to the prisoner and to society, as the very worst system ever devised or tolerated.

No candid or liberal mind will confound any system prescribed and adopted, with the *mode* in which such system is carried into daily operation. What person, acquainted with the horrible abuses, and the bloody atrocities, which at times, within a few years, have blackened the annals of the prisons at Auburn, Mt. Pleasant, &c. will be justified, either by his own conscience, or the public, in passing a sweeping censure upon the systems on which these, and other populous prisons are established. The fact is, that, in all prisons every where, cruelties on the one hand, and injudicious laxity of discipline on the other, have at times appeared, and will at intervals be renewed, except the most vigilant oversight is maintained. A fruitful source of these evils may be traced to the frequent change of the governing officers, according as one political party or the other gains ascendency. It is too often that men are appointed, not for their peculiar fitness for governing prisoners, and conducting the financial concerns of the establishment, so much as to serve political ends, and satisfy narrow local prejudices. This is especially the fact in relation to the second class of officers in the penitentiaries, the keepers of the county prisons, and the masters of the alms-houses. Many of them are excellent men, honest, and industrious ; many are of that class which is often called ' well-meaning men,' and capable in pirvate life of filling their station with respectability. But, as rulers of other men, placed in a situation of authority to restrain, to command, and to direct, they lack knowledge and experience of human nature, and tact and adaptation by natural and improved capacities, for the grave and responsible duties of governing their *fellow-men ;* and not only of governing men, but those who are the most ignorant and most perverted.

Heretofore the exceeding importance of selecting officers by their moral gifts and fitness, not merely to maintain outward discipline, but to promote the substantial, lasting good of the prisoner, has been often overlooked, or regarded as a secondary consideration. But that character is not, in its general, social acceptation lost sight of, is revealed in the fact that, for at least fifteen years past, the standard for the choice of the head officers of prisons in the United States has been rising, and it is mainly to this that the progressive improvement in prisons, gradual as it has been, may be ascribed. In proportion as these offices are made honorable and respectable,—I mean not only the offices of chief warden, but those of second and third rank, —in both the penitentiaries and county jails, will competent and respectable men be found to conduct these institutions. I would not have the officers become preachers; I would not have them much interfere with the religious teaching, so called, of the prisoners ; but I would have them all moral guides ; and, while I would not desire to see them always, nor very often, engaged in discoursing and formal lecturing, I would have all they both say and do produce an encouraging, awakening, and enlightening effect upon the prisoner. A few words are more likely to do good, than a tedious lesson; the too little regarded influences of manner, tone, and expression, are the most efficient help to all prisoners, whether amongst 'the silent,' 'the separate,' or 'the congregated classes.' In order to do good, a man must be good; and he will not be good except he have instruction by counsel and by example. Now who have the power of exercising these direct hourly influences, except the officers who have charge of the prisons and of the prisoners? It is the word *in season*, and *fitly spoken*, which may kindle a desire in the degraded to retrieve himself. The faint desire becomes quickened into a living purpose; this passes into the fixed resolve; and this creates a sentiment of self-respect. Self-respect implanted, conducts to the desire of possessing the respect and confidence of others; and through these paths grow up moral sentiments, gradually increasing and gaining strength; and, in time, there is the more profound and soul-saving sentiment of reverence for God, acknowledgment of his laws, and a truer perception of that sanctifying knowledge which causeth not to err.

If it is a fatal mistake to appoint incompetent officers to fill the very responsible stations just alluded to, it is a yet more fatal error in the community to demand rotation in office, annually or biennially. A really competent officer should not be displaced, but by his own request; for, granting his successor to be also well qualified, he will have less ability to conduct the discipline of prisoners, since he will want the habit and knowledge which result from experience only, and which no merely general good dispositions can supply. I do not wish to convey the idea that this should be a life-office; far from it. I have never conversed with officers of the least habit of reflection, who do not say that the office of a prison-keeper, who comes constantly in direct contact with prisoners, tends to blunt the moral susceptibilities. The trial and discipline of the dispositions, and of the habits of prison officers, are too severe to be permitted to spread over a whole life; five or ten years, without interval, is perhaps as long a period for holding these offices as the keepers should desire, or as would really prove advantageous to the institution.

I have not leisure to enlarge upon the finance of the penitentiaries; the subject has been elaborately, rather than ably discussed, and variously rather than practically reported; and, it seems to me, with less advantage to institutions and the community, than any topic connected with prison affairs. It is desirable that penitentiaries should not be a cost to government; on the other hand they should not be a source of profit. If the mechanic arts can be conducted with such diligence and success as to exceed the demand for the prison expenses, it would be well to apply the surplus to increasing the means of moral and general instruction for the prisoners, by establishing and maintaining libraries of well chosen books; by multiplying discreet and earnest teachers, and by apportioning a part of every day for giving and receiving instruction. A considerable revenue has been derived at some prisons by 'admission money,' that is, receiving at the entrance the sum of twenty-five cents each, from numerous visitors. This should not be allowed. None but official visitors, and persons who visit prisons for some definite objects connected with the administration of these establishments, and such of the relatives or friends of the prisoner, as by law have the liberty to be admitted, ought to be received. All who go to gratify a mere curiosity, 'to see the place, and to see how the prisoners look,' should be excluded. The effect of this indiscriminate exposure upon the prisoner is bad, or, if it does not injure him, it only proves that he is so hardened in guilt, and so debased, that in being made a spectacle for the gratification of the thoughtless and the curious, he is willing his degradation should be as public as his life has been debased. Of this class there are not many.

At the expiration of a sentence, it is customary, in all the States, to discharge the prisoner decently clothed, and supplied with a small sum of money, usually varying from three to five dollars. If a prisoner have friends and home near, this is sufficient; but this is not oftenest nor often the case; and this usual provision is quite inadequate to convey the convict to a distant home, to a place of business, or long to support him honestly while he seeks an employer and employment; and

which, as a graduate from a State prison, he obtains not without
encountering many difficulties and repulses, if indeed his efforts
do not end in total disappointment; so that, discouraged and
tempted, he returns to old associates and associations, and
betakes himself again to those law-deriding modes of life that
shortly subject him to misery and disgrace, if not to a speedy
incarceration in the county jail.

The disadvantages under which prisoners labour upon enlargement, have within a few years, gradually awakened the
attention of the humane and benevolent; and, in New York,
within the last year, a society has been formed, styled ' the
Prison Association of New York,' which projects, under an
extremely comprehensive series of by-laws, the most extensive
and thorough prison reforms; and, amongst many special objects, the relief of enlarged convicts is proposed, ' by keeping
an office in the city of New York, where discharged prisoners
may apply for aid and advice ; ' by endeavoring to procure good
boarding-places for the discharged prisoners, where they will
not be exposed to corrupting influences,—by taking care not to
have more than one in one place, when it can be avoided ;'
' and seeing that the prisoners are provided with suitable clothing, of a kind that will not attract attention, and point them out
as convicts.' An enlightened and excellent spirit has charac-
terised the first movements of this Association ; but in order to
realize these aims, it is necessary that not one, nor three, nor
five members should take an active part in the work : the many
are needed ; and in order to produce satisfactory results, over
so wide a field of various labor, a concentration of influence
and action is necessary, which will demand the undivided devotion of the time and energy of many of those who give their
names to this great cause.

I believe the best mode of aiding convicts is, so to apportion
their tasks in prison, as to give to the industrious the opportunity of earning a sum for themselves by ' over-work.' A man
usually values that most for which he has labored ; he uses
that most frugally which he has toiled hour by hour and day
by day to acquire. I believe every convict will be disposed to
make a better use of the money he earns, than of that he
receives gratuitously. He who works for his maintenance has

a higher sense of self-respect, than he who receives his support from others. No man is so quickly and so certainly brought low in his own or others' esteem, as the common pauper. Indulged habits of dependence create habits of indolence, and indolence opens the portal to petty errors, to many degrading habits, and to vice and crime with their attendant train of miseries.

The prison societies in Philadelphia have, for many years, devoted a portion of the funds, derived from annual subscriptions, to the relief of prisoners discharged from the penitentiaries. At this time the system of over-work is adopted in the Eastern Penitentiary, and it is from a knowledge of the benefits resulting from this, together with previous observation of a want to be supplied in some way in other States, that I should strongly recommend this practice.

It is not to be supposed that all who are the inmates of prisons will be capable of earning their own support, and still less of accomplishing over-work, whereby a sum may be accumulated against the day of need. There is in every prison a large number of feeble, infirm, and incompetent persons, who have so small capacity that their earnings at most are trifling. Still, if these feeble, inefficient persons do all they can; if they behave well, and are disposed to observe the rules of discipline, they might receive some small allowance, so that encouragement might be given to quicken industry, and they too might have some honestly-earned savings, as a resource when discharged. I am confident it is neither a true direction of charity, nor is it real kindness, to give considerable sums of money to this class of persons.

Some persons advocate the systems of *rewards* in prison for a term of good conduct or for special diligence. Any supposed advantage from this plan would be overbalanced by increased difficulties of discipline. Jealousies and quarrels would arise ; the judgment of the ward-officer would be at fault, and insubordination would follow. The more simple and direct the system of government, the more easily will discipline be maintained. Complex rules and measures, like complex machinery, are often out of order. This system, a few years since, was restorted to in some of the French prisons and at Lausanne, and proved totally impracticable.

Punishments have been much discussed, and with results but little satisfactory. Some advocate a stern rule of despotism, sustained by the use of chains, and the application of that compound instrument of torture, jeeringly called by officials ' the cat,' or ' cat o' nine ;' others, with a morbid sensibility, nourished at the expense of discreet judgment, as well as true humanity, would forbid to the executive officers of prisons all means of discipline, except the language of persuasion.

That period may arrive when this so beautiful and sensible influence may be all that is needed, but at present those who urge the abandonment of all modes of maintaining discipline besides this, must be either reckless of consequences, or ignorant of human nature as manifested by a considerable portion of ignorant, long-abased convicts. Those, who discover few traits above the lowest of the brute creation, can no more, *at first*, be influenced to observe rules and general order by mild influence and words, than the tiger or hyena can be brought to tameness by an expressive word or gentle regard. This subject cannot here be fully discussed, and therefore cannot be accurately understood, except by those who have learnt by often and long-time observation, the various mental and moral conditions of convicts. I am certain that I could never subdue my instinctive horror and disgust of punishment by the lash, as a means of producing submission and obedience. I could never order, witness, or permit its application ; but I am forced, with unspeakable reluctance, to concede, that I believe it may be sometimes *the only* mode, under the Auburn, or congregated system, by which an insurrectionary spirit can be conquered. Punishment should never be inflicted by the order of an inferior officer, nor through his sole representation. It should not be inflicted during the first moments of excitement, when the offence is committed ; it should not be inflicted till reasonable and mild measures have been persevered in, and proved to be unavailing ; it should, in the strictest, most literal sense, be the *dernier resort.*

The *gag* is another form of punishment, which seems to me shocking and extremely objectionable ; yet it is sometimes employed. Twice, some years since, it was used upon an incorrigible prisoner in the Eastern Penitentiary, but never was con-

sidered a usual means of discipline. A letter addressed to the
Warden of the prison at Sing Sing, August 1844, inquiring
somewhat concerning present discipline, was very satisfactorily
and fully replied to by one of the Inspectors, the Hon. J.
W. Edmonds; who, speaking of the modes of punishment,
remarks,

"The gag has been sometimes applied, but it has been only among
the females that it has been rendered *absolutely* necessary! The
number of punishments inflicted, in the Sing Sing prison, during three
months from April 1 to July 1, 1844, was as follows—there being 868
prisoners in the men's prison—in April, 113 flogged ; in May, 94 ; in
June, 107. There being 73 prisoners in the women's prison—in April,
13 punishments ; May, 11 ; June, 7." The least number of lashes at
a time with the cat 6, the largest number at one time I did not learn.
"In the men's prison the form of punishment is by the lash. This
mode of punishment is regarded by the present Inspectors as so excep-
tionable, that they are resorting to every means in their power to super-
sede it. The prison was constructed under the direction of one who
would recognise no other mode of government, and consequently no
provision was made for any other mode. The present Inspectors com-
plained of this, in their last report to the Legislature ; but no notice
was taken of it, and they have therefore, with such means as was in
their power,—much straightened by the deranged condition of the
finances of the prison,—adopted means to do away with the lash.
They are now erecting an outer ward, to contain sixteen solitary cells,
for the purpose of punishing the refractory. These will soon be completed ; and then the mode of punishment will be deprivation of food,
or of bed, shower-bath, solitary confinement, and confinement in a dark
cell. The three former are already used, and have reduced the amount
of punishments with the lash.
"In the women's prison, the lash is never used. There the punishments are confinement to their own cells in the main dormitory, or in
separate cells, with reduction of food, ' and the application of the gag.' "

In the Maryland prison, the lash is resorted to for the women ;
but, from all I observed and learnt, I should judge with but
little permanent advantage.

Wishing to learn what was the success of the amelioration in
discipline, referred to by Judge Edmonds, I revisited the prison
at Sing Sing, in November, and found the governors of both
the men and women's prison determined to maintain order
through the mildest possible influences ; but all their exertions,
up to that time, had not exempted them from the painful duty
of imposing severe measures ; but the record for October and

November, furnished to me by the Warden last December, will show the then state of discipline.

The following is an extract from the letter referred to :—

" I send to you the record of the number of punishments with the lash in the month of October, 1844. It is proper for me to remark, however, that we resort to the lash only when milder punishments have been applied without securing submission to our discipline.

By keeper H.—J. W., 8 lashes, for destroying property and leaving his work. J. M. C., 8 lashes, for stealing, laughing, and talking. J. J., 10, for destroying property.

By keeper Sh.—H. B., 10 lashes, for stealing files and making ' bone-work.' L. C., 10, for talking, and leaving the shop without leave. H. N., 10, for having prohibited articles in his cell.

By keeper J.—R. H., 6, for making a noise in his cell. C. F. J., 10, for insolence and falsehood.

By keeper Sd.—J. S., 15, for noise and talking in his cell. J. H., 15, for spoiling his work.

By keeper T.—H. F., 15, not doing his work—*and not well*. N. M., 6, for not doing his work. S. P., 7, for talking.

By keeper A.—M. W. D., 10 lashes, for singing in his cell.

By keeper L.—J. C., 8, for talking.

By keeper R.—A. H., 8, for talking loud in his cell. W. P., 6, for the like offence.

By keeper V. W.—L. L., 10, for profane language, &c.

By keeper G.—A. B., 20, for assault on keeper, and insolence.

By keeper M.—W. H. P., 13, for insolence and profanity.

By keeper S.—H. F., 8, for violation of shop rules.

By keeper K.—J. N., 10, making loud noise in his cell.

By keeper W.—P. F., 12, for stealing, and destroying property.

By keeper Ma.—W. D., 12, talking and disobedience.

By keeper C.—G. B., 8, stealing yarn and trafficking.

Making 255 lashings inflicted on 25 men this month ; 54 convicts violated the rules either of the prison or the shops, who have received punishments substituted for the lash ; aggregate of violations, 79. A great diminution since April, May, and June.

In the month of November, 1844, *twenty-five* convicts received punishment with the lash, amounting to 296 blows with " *the cat*," making an increase of 41 lashes for the following violations of discipline :—

6 for assaults upon their fellow prisoners.

3 for refusing to work, 2 for singing, and 2 for talking.

7 for talking and insolence ; 1 an attempt to escape, and insolence ; 2, spoiling their work ; 1 for maiming himself three times, to avoid labor :—in all 25.

Punished the same month, without the lash, 30.
Making an aggregate of 55 for violations of rules."

More recently than the above I have the following official report :—

"In consequence of a more judicious exercise of discipline in the Sing Sing prison, 1844–45, the number of *lashes* in the men's prison has diminished from *one thousand one hundred and ninety-five* (1195) per month, to about two hundred." As each lash is *inflicted* with the ' *cat o' nine*,' there appears to have been *ten thousand seven hundred and fifty-five strokes.* "The number of offences against discipline has decreased from *one hundred and thirty*, per month, to fifty, and in the women's prison, from forty-seven, per month, to eleven."

With nearly 1,000 convicts, viz. 868 men, and 73 women, on the ' silent,' congregated system, governed by a few officers, and restrained by a few guards outside the prison, the prison itself not enclosed by walls, and where communication permitted would assure rebellion, and slight breaches of discipline afford opportunities for conversation and plotting, I am compelled to admit that the only security of the prison, and safety of the officers, is in the most careful discipline, and in the officers who administer discipline. Even granting the remission of discipline, as now permitted in the Massachusetts prison to prove successful in continued practice, at Sing Sing, for years to come, it would be totally impracticable. It was attempted in the Connecticut prison and failed, when the convicts numbered less than 200.

The officers at Sing Sing certainly deserve high praise for their efforts during the past year, at establishing and maintaining a mild form of discipline. Difficulties and serious obstacles present themselves continually. Here is the most corrupt, the most degraded, most desperate class of prisoners, in any prison north of Mason and Dixon's line. Coming, as they chiefly do, from the city of New York, and from a corrupting apprenticeship in that most corrupting city-prison, the Tombs, where hundreds congregate, and communicate and receive evil influences continually, how should it be otherwise? And this too is through no fault of the officers, since the internal construction and arrangements of the prison prevent separation.

The Prison Association may in time procure at least a partial remedy for some of these destroying evils.

I sincerely believe that La Force never admitted more widely corrupting influences, nor Newgate greater and more destructive ones, than are disseminated in the Tombs. I refer entirely to the moral condition, especially in the men's prison. Wholesome changes have been introduced into the women's apartments and cells, but the moral miasma is diffused throughout; free association neutralizes all efforts to instruct and reclaim.

A second great disadvantage under which the officers labor at Sing Sing, and also in this respect the officers at Auburn, is the very large number brought upon one ground. It is much less difficult and hazardous to introduce changes, and to relax discipline in the New England prisons, and in those of the Southern States, which are governed on the same system, than in the Penitentiaries of New York, where the lives of guards and officers are in imminent danger from these desperate convicts, if discipline be relaxed, and indulgences introduced. One thing is sure, this can never be done here to the extent the superior officers and inspectors desire, and which society hopes and asks, till the prisons and prisoners are in these two establishments subdivided, and much additional provision made for their moral instruction, and well-directed religious teaching. The wonder is, that so accurate discipline is maintained at these several prisons, when one considers the limited physical force, and extremely partial moral influences, which are brought to bear on them. It must not be forgotten that even in the prisons where there are fewer convicts, and where the Auburn system has been said to be well administered, dangerous conspiracies have been plotted, and valuable lives have been sacrificed in repeated instances by desperate convicts.

From the Warden of the state prison at Auburn, I received a letter dated July 17, 1844, replying to inquiries on the subject of punishments of which the following is a brief extract :—

" No convict has been in solitary confinement for any punishment since April 1 ; the number of punishments inflicted was, in April, 74 ; May, 67 ; June, 69 ; the number of convicts at that time ranging from 768 to 826. There are but very few cases when more than six blows are required to enforce submission. In some aggravated cases twelve blows are inflicted with the cat, and one convict, a desperate robber and burglar, received 41 blows, and has since behaved well. Punishment with cold water has been most effectual, in subduing the refractory, but I believe is often detrimental to health, and has therefore been discontinued at this prison. Close confinement is injurious and uncertain in its effects. I should resort to it if reasonable flogging proved insufficient. After much anxious reflection I have come to the conclusion, that moderate punishment with the cat, producing temporary smart, without permanent injury, is the most consistent with true humanity. Where this punishment has been carried to excess, as has been at times the case in former years, both mind and health were permanently injured."

I was at Auburn in November following the date of this letter, the refractory convict above referred to had cunningly planned a conspiracy a week or two before, associated with other desperate prisoners, which was nigh being successful, and which involved the life of every officer on the grounds. Conspiracies at Sing Sing and other prisons have in like manner been plotted, but as yet timely discovered, usually through the faint-heartedness of some of the associates. It is to the fear of mutual betrayal, the little confidence one can place in his fellow, that the security of the large prisons is mainly ascribable.

A communication from the Warden of the prison at Wethersfield, contains the following passage on punishments :—

" We use the solitary cell for a short time, keeping the prisoner upon bread and water, and in some cases we punish with stripes. But with us very little punishment of any kind is found necessary ; the *power* possessed by the officer to inflict it, serves to prevent transgression. There were but two prisoners punished in the month of April, four in May, and none in June; the whole number of prisoners at the time being 180, of which 46 were black, and 21 were women. After an experience of twenty years, watching the effect and influence of state prison detention and discipline upon criminals, I am constrained to say, that its effect in general has not been to reform those who *in early life have been disposed to crime*, even when the best opportunities have been afforded to them for reformation."

I have visited the Penitentiary, above referred to, three times within a year ; those at Auburn, Sing Sing, Baltimore, and Concord twice ; those in Virginia, District of Columbia, Ohio, Rhode Island, and Pittsburg once ; that of Massachusetts several times; and those at Philadelphia and Trenton by more than twenty different visits within the same period. The discipline at Baltimore is good ; the punishments, according to numbers, less than at Sing Sing; also less at Washington and at Richmond. At Rhode-Island rarely inflicted, but the number of prisoners is less than twenty! At Concord fewer punishments than in former years. At Columbus and at Charlestown the Wardens severally, are men who entered on their office with the earnest desire to do away all punishment, and they had faith in being able to accomplish their truly benevolent wishes. Neither has realised his anticipations. The punishments are indeed of late not numerous nor excessive in either ; a very gentle application of cold water at Columbus was all the punishment which had been inflicted for months before I was there, in August, 1844. The Warden has sent me his last report, which contains the following remarks on this subject :—

" It has been my constant aim to avoid, as much as possible, all un-necessary severity, and especially to use the *lash* as sparingly as possible. As a substitute for this mode of punishment, I have constructed a *shower bath*, which in most cases I have found more efficient and less severe. For the last nine months I have suffered no punishment of any kind to be inflicted (except in extraordinary cases) unless upon mature deliberation it proved indispensably necessary. Nor has any been inflicted except in my presence. To be always present I consider important, not only for the purpose of directing what measure of punishment should be inflicted, but to impress upon the offender the fact, that his punishment having been inflicted under the eye, and by the direction of the principal officer, there can be no appeal from his decision,— and no greater punishment inflicted than is sanctioned by the Warden."

The lash is reluctantly or infrequently resorted to at Charlestown ; and, as the Warden lately told me, ' only when all other modes of influence totally fail ;' but the discipline is lax in the extreme, and it will be perceived by reference to the tables furnished to me by the clerk and Warden, that since the prison-rules have been modified or dispensed with, as time advances, the difficulty of preserving order and assuring obedience has increased.

Punishments in the Massachusetts State Prison, in April, May, and June, 1844 and '45 ;—

Date. APRIL, 1844.	OFFENCE.	Days Stripes. Solitary.
For talking repeatedly, and insolence	. . .	1
" gross disobedience of orders	. . .	1

Date.	Offence.	Stripes.	Days. Solitary
April, 1844,			
For insolence and disobedience of orders			1
" attempting to obtain tobacco			1½
" obstinately refusing to labor		1	
" refusing to labor			1
" insolence to an officer			1
April, 1845.			
For making a disturbance in his shop			1
" insolence to an officer			1
" obtaining tobacco from a visitor			3
" insolence to his officer			2
" disobedience and insolence			1
" making a disturbance in his shop			2
" quarrelling with a fellow convict			2
" insolence and disobedience of orders			2
" making a disturbance in his shop and cell			2
" attempting to break out of his cell			1½
" insolence to his officer			1
" threatening his officer with violence		4	
May, 1844.			
For profane language and insolence		3	
" gross insolence to an officer			1
" refusing to labor			2
" disobedience of orders and leaving his shop		1	
" gross insolence and disturbing the quiet of solitary prison		8	
" insolence and profanity		3	
" insolence to an officer			1
" insolence and disobedience of orders			1
May, 1845.			
For quarrelling with a convict			1½
" assaulting a fellow convict			1
" quarrelling with a fellow convict			1
" secreting himself with intent to escape		5	1
" gross insolence and disobedience			2
" do. do do			3
" gross insolence and insubordination			2
" do to his officer			2
" assaulting and striking a convict		7	
" quarrelling with a fellow convict			1½
" gross insolence to his officer			1
" inattention to his work, &c.			2
June, 1844.			
For disobedience of express orders			1
" disobedience and insubordination			2
" disturbing the quiet of the solitary prison		6	
" insolence to an officer			2
" quarrelling with and striking a fellow prisoner		6	
June, 1845.			
For refusing to labor			1

Date, JUNE, 1845, continued. OFFENCES.		Days Stripes. Solitary.
For making a noise while in his cell		1
" idleness and gross insolence		4
" quarrelling with a fellow convict		2
" making a noise while in his cell		1
" quarrelling with a fellow convict		2
" gross insolence to an officer		2
" disobedience of orders		1
" gross insolence to an officer		2
" do and disobedience		3
" refusing to labour and hiding his tools		4
" disobedience of orders and gross insolence	5	
" gross insolence to his officer		2
" insolence, disobedience and idleness	8	
" making a disturbance while in his cell		1
" insolence and having prohibited articles		$1\frac{1}{2}$
" making a disturbance in his cell		1
" do do while in his cell		1
" quarrelling with a fellow convict		2
" gross insolence to an officer	3	
" refusing to labour		1
" making a disturbance while in his cell		1
" fighting with a fellow convict		2
" gross laziness and inattention to work		1
" refusing to labour		1

The system of indulgence often works well for a few months, and possibly for a year or two, that is, the officers have to contend with no special difficulties. But I never have known any prison in which discipline is much dispensed with, which has not fallen into confusion, and in which it could be found that the good of the convicts has eventually, either morally or physically, been promoted. *Rules must be established and enforced,* and, as numbers are increased in prisons, the *necessity* for vigilance increases. These rules, let it be understood, may be *kindly* while firmly enforced. I would never suffer any exhibition of ill-temper, or an arbitrary exercise of authority. *The officers should be equally subject to rules and discipline as the prisoners.*

I fear that the Inspectors, and also the Warden and Chaplain of the Massachusetts prison, have been somewhat too hasty in their conclusions in dispensing with some observances and rules generally connected with discipline, and that their congratulations to each other and the public, as expressed in the last two annual reports, are based on their wishes and hopes, rather than on a knowledge of prison government and its necessities. I respect in them the *feeling* which has prompted the wish to dispense with *forms*, and the *appearance* of restraint, and some close rules ; I lament the necessity of imposing them ; but I am, from a four years' observation of jails and penitentiaries, obliged to allow, that greater restraints are necessary in all these, than our wishes, putting aside reasoning on consequences, would determine. *Steady, firm,* and *kind* government of prisoners is the truest humanity, and the best exercise of duty. It is with convicts as with children ; unseasonable indulgence indiscreetly granted, leads to mischiefs which we may deplore but cannot repair.

What would be called discipline, in most prisons on the Auburn plan in the United States, is, at Charlestown and at Columbus, exceedingly lax, especially at the former. The men do not infringe rules as often perhaps as at Sing Sing ; but it is because they are dispensed with. There is no State prison at present between the Canadas on the north, and the Carolinas and Tennessee on the south, where so much freedom is enjoyed as at Charlestown. Next after this is the prison at Columbus ; and thirdly the prison at Windsor, Ver. With the exception of Rhode Island prison, which has so few prisoners that one can hardly make a comparison with others, the most correct and humane discipline, because the best order amongst equal numbers, with fewest punishments, is at Weathersfield. This prison is remarkable for the thorough neatness, and good arrangement of every part and department. The chief defect is, the too little time given to moral instruction, and too little time to the prisoners for reading and self-improvement : this is a defect common to every prison on the ' silent or Auburn system' in the land ; and also to the prison at South Trenton, New Jersey, which is on the ' separate' or Pennsylvania system. On this subject I am satisfied juster views are breaking upon the public mind, and I believe we may reasonably look for important and highly advantageous changes in the prisons throughout the United States within the next ten years ; but the first and most needed reforms are in the county jails or detaining prisons.

Corporal punishment is permitted by law in the Rhode-Island prison, since they have abandoned the ' separate system,' or, as they called it, the ' solitary system ;' ' greater stimulants to fear of punishment being needed, as they report, under the congregated labor system, as now adopted.' The punishments in Thomaston, Maine, and in Windsor, Vermont, were mild and not frequent when I was last at these prisons, two years since ; the discipline of the latter measuring near that at Columbus, but less relaxed than that at Charlestown. The punishment at the Eastern Penitentiary and at the Western Penitentiary, Pennsylvania, and the prison at South Trenton, established on the ' separate system,' are, placing the offender in an unfurnished cell, without employment, and if very refractory by chaining, and reducing the food, as at Auburn and Sing Sing ; but the temptations to break rules, and disturb the general arrangements of the prisons, are so few, that discipline is maintained without difficulty, and very few are brought at all under punishment, even that of withdrawing a single meal ; an admonition from the Warden or the Inspectors, or counsel from the moral instructors, is almost all that is requisite.

Punishments in the Eastern Penitentiary, in the months of April, May, and June, 1844, as copied from the Prison Records :—

" Mode—confinement in a cell, the window of which is darkened by a blanket being thrown over the glass ; food—one and a quarter pounds of good wheat bread per day ; water at command ; visited by physician daily ; size of the cell 14 ft. 10½ in. long, 7 ft. 6 in. wide ; average height 11 ft. 8 in. The punishments were as follows :—

1 prisoner in solitary cell for 9 hours—2 for 3 days—3 for 4 days— 1 for 6 days—4 for 7 days— making 11 punishments.
1 prisoner on 1¼ lb. wheat bread, and water, in ordinary cell, 7 days, making 12 punishments in 11 prisoners.
Average number in confinement, 366.
Punishments of the same description, in darkened cell, in April, May, and June, 1845 :—
1 prisoner for 1 day—5 for 3 days—4 for 4 days—1 for 5 days— 2 for 6 days—total 13.
Average number of prisoners, 311.
Irons are used on the wrists and ancles when necessary ; the physician visits them daily, *and changes the diet if he thinks best, on account of health ;* a record is exhibited twice each week to the visiting inspectors, who regularly visit those under confinement. The punish-

ments in this prison are restricted, by the rules to the above mode only, and the duration of time limited to one week ; the power of punishing is confined to the warden's orders.

The rule I have adopted, and found to be best, (writes the warden,) is, for the *first offences* to release the prisoner as soon as he promises amendment ; this plan is proved to be best, by the few second offences.

The Punishments for six months, Jan., Feb., and March, including the months of April, May, and June, 1845, as above recorded were :—
Darkened cell—1 day, 1 ; 2 days, 5 ; 3 days, 10 ; 4 days, 4 ; 5 days, 6 ; 6 days, 3 ; 7 days, 8. Total, 37.

Punishments 37 in the persons of 34 prisoners, in six months.

Average number of convicts, for six months, 316."

In addition to the desciplinary punishments at Trenton, the wardens, with the concurrence of the inspectors, at a former period, adopted the *douche* or bolt-bath, as once used at Auburn ; but it was abandoned, for the same reasons which, as already stated, led to its disuse there. Though punishments are rare, the discipline at Trenton, for the last few years, has been unequal. The best advantages of the system are not as yet fully possessed here. There is a great deficiency of moral instruction at present : in fact there has never been any sufficient nor any authorized legislative provision to meet these wants of the convicts.

If we must concede to the prisons, which are established on the ' silent system,' as in Massachusetts, Rhode Island, and Maryland, the use of the lash, ' when all other means fail,' we should urge that, every where, this terrible necessity be determined only by the principal officer of the prison ; and that, under no circumstances, it be permitted to the officers of the watch, or of the shops, to adjudge and inflict the punishment. I have not perceived latterly, at any of the prisons, any disposition on the part of the officers to abuse their power ; but on the contrary an evident desire to carry into effect a milder rule ; still it is too great a temptation, and too responsible a power to allow to the large class of second officers the liberty of judging, pronouncing sentence, and executing the penalty of disobedience upon the prisoners under their charge.

I am convinced that, with due care, and under proper direction, the shower-bath, (not the *douche*, or bolt bath,) is a very effectual means of procuring submission to proper rules and regulations. It is a mode of discipline which may be, and which has been abused, but so has and may be every other form of punishment which the law allows; and it is quite certain that while corrective force is needed for the government of prisons, the Warden must be armed with discretionary authority; and I think most prisoners would yield as readily to a shower procured by a single bucket of water, as by a dozen lashes : the lash hardens a hard nature, and degrades a degraded one. So various are the tempers and characters of convicts, that there can properly be no one prescribed form of correction ; one prisoner yields to kind expostulation the moment after excitement has subsided, another will dread the shower-bath, another the lash, another his unfurnished, comfortless cell ; a few, a very few, will dread nothing. It may be well that these should be quite separated from others, and employed apart till a steady moral instruction may so have softened, and raised, and enlightened them, that they shall be capable of sharing their work and time with others.

While we diminish the stimulant of *fear*, we must increase to prisoners the incitements of *hope :* in proportion as we extinguish the *terrors* of the law, we should awaken and strengthen the *control* of the *conscience.* While, governed by humanity, we place the prisoner under the fewest possible restraints, and multiply the decent comforts of a well-ordered life, we must so impress him with a sense of their value, as to displace habits of indolence and personal neglect. Man is not made better by being degraded; he is seldom restrained from crime by harsh measures, except the principle of fear predominates in his character; and then he is never made radically better for its influence.

I earnestly plead for mild measures in governing the bad, the corrupt; and not the less urgently, *because* it is to the defects of our social organization, to the multiplied, and multiplying temptations to crime, in fact, it is to our wealth and prosperity, and to our very civilization, that we chiefly owe the increase of evil-doers. In the exercise of justice, let mercy too have sway, but mercy not commingled with morbid sensibilities and unwholesome, untimely sympathy ; the injudicious

4

indulgence of these false sentiments tends to establish the criminal in criminal purposes, and to confirm the vicious in vicious propensities.

DURATION OF SENTENCES.—Insubordination is stimulated, and efforts for reform often rendered abortive, by the injudicious infliction of *long periods* of imprisonment. There is often great disproportion between the offence and the punishment, and the punishment and the offence. Men have an innate sense of justice. Even individuals of very weak understanding, and but little instructed, have a perception of the distinctions of a just award between crime and its penalty. Mr. Morgan, the Warden of the Penitentiary at Richmond, reports, that the infliction of long sentences of ten, twelve, fifteen, and seventeen years, for crimes less than murder, render his prisoners obstinate, irritable, and often desperate. This sentiment is generally concurred in by those officers in prisons, who have had experience and time to observe the effects of such punishments. Nothing is more common even among the *officers* who are placed immediately over the prisoners to direct their labor, than the expression of distrust of the administration of justice, a sentiment which grows out of the observation of the great inequality in sentences pronounced for the same offences, on men equal in moral condition. Convicts become reckless and obstinate, and callous to all influences moral or religious, when subject to extreme terms of imprisonment.

Of 205 prisoners in the Richmond prison, Sept. 1842, 48 were under sentence for periods of ten years and more. Of 213 in prison in Sept. 1843, 55 were under sentences of extreme duration, exceeding ten years.

Of 150 prisoners committed to the penitentiary in Columbus, Ohio, in 12 months, 1842, 21 were for terms of ten years and over ; 5 being for 17 years.

In the Maryland prison, in 1843, 8 were received for terms of ten years ; and in 1844, 7 were received for ten years and over.

In 1840, there were, in the Massachusetts Penitentiary, 47 whose terms of sentence exceeded ten years ; of this number 14 were for life. In 1844, there were 42 ; 12 being for life, and 1 for 35 years.

Of 57 convicts in the prison at Thomaston, Jan. 1843, 6 were for life (1 only for murder) and 5 for more than 10 years ; making 11 for long periods of time.

In the Windsor prison, Jan. 1844, were 67 convicts—5 were for time beyond 10 years.

At the Concord prison, of 89 convicts in June 1844, 12 were for life, 1 for 22 years, and 8 for terms over ten years and under 15. Of these 21 convicts, 3 were charged with murder in the second degree, 2 with attempt to murder, and 2 with manslaughter.

At the Wethersfield prison, March 1845, of 197 convicts, there were 17 for life, 7 for 15 years, 6 for 10 years, 3 with fines in addition ; 3 for 20 years ; 10 for periods ranging from 12 to 15 years ; 7 for 9 years ; 10 for 8 years ; and 10 for 7 years.

In the Providence prison, Oct. 1844, of 20 convicts, 3 were for life, (1 since pardoned) 1 for 15 years, and 1 for 8 years.

In the Sing Sing prison, Nov. 1844, of 868 men convicts, 9 were in for life ; 10 for over 20 years ; 39 for between 10 and 20 years ; 85 for 10 years ; 8 for 9½ years ; 6 for 9 years. Of 73 women convicts, 11 were from 7 to 10 years, and 2 over 10 ; none for life.

In the Auburn prison, Jan. 1845, of 778 convicts, 10 were sentenced for life ; but the periods of sentence for the others were not recorded in the report. In the report for 1842, of 712 convicts, 58 were from 10 to 20 years ; 240 from 5 to 10 years ; 4 to 20 years and over ; 7 for life.

In the Trenton prison, 1844, of 159 convicts, 1 was for life, 1 for 20 and 3 for 15 years ; 1 for 12 ; 1 for 14 ; and 9 for 10 years ;— making 16 for ten years and over.

In the Western Penitentiary, Alleghany city, 1841, of 130 convicts, 8 were for ten years and over.

In the Eastern Penitentiary, Philadelphia, 1841, of 126 convicts, 1 was sentenced to 8 years, 2 to 9 years, 2 to 10 years, 4 to 12 years. Of 142 convicted in 1842, 3 were for 7 years, 6 for 10 years, 1 for 11 years, 1 for 13 years, 1 for 18 years, 1 for 19 years, 1 for 20 years, and 1 for 21 years—making 12 in one year for terms exceeding ten years. Of 156 convicts received in 1843, 6 were for 7 years, 4 for 10 years, 1 for 12 years, and 3 for 15 years. In 1844, of 138 convicts received, 3 were for 7 years and over ; 1 for nine, 3 for ten, and 2 for 12 years.

PARDONS AND THE PARDONING POWER.—' Crimes,' says Montesquieu, ' are more frequently prevented by the *certainty*, than by the severity of punishment.'

Of what use is it to enact laws for the security of society ; to institute courts of justice for the execution of them ; to organize an active police force, and establish municipal regulations?— of what use to construct county prisons, and build vast penitentiaries,—if arrests, and trials, and convictions, and sentences, are so frequently followed by unconditional pardons, as to have produced, throughout our country, such assured belief amongst all classes of offenders that many chances are in favor of their escape from condign punishment, even in the event of arrest, trial, and conviction? So frequently and indiscriminately has the pardoning power been exercised, in many of the States, during the last twenty years, that nothing is so common, when first a prisoner is conducted to prison, as the bold expression and confident expectation of speedy enlargement. Either friends have promised to intercede, or legal advisers have encouraged the idea, or reliance on the executive is sanguine, and the prisoner goes to his cell, or the work-shop, not in a frame of mind to obey the rules of the prison, not disposed to apply himself to assigned employments, not directing his thoughts to repentance and future good purposes, but determined to resist wholesome influences, and cultivate indifference or obstinacy. I speak of the majority of convicts; there are always exceptions; there are some who are not confirmed in criminal habits, and who have committed felonies while under peculiar trials and temptations. The claims of these to merciful consideration should not be put aside, to make place for importunities in favor of the basest of offenders.

The wardens of the prisons have, for years, testified against the extreme and injudicious exercise of the pardoning power; increasing, as it does in the prisons, the difficulty of subordination, and indisposing the prisoners to learn the several trades at which they are placed in a manner to produce merchantable work. The courts have censured, and communities have remarked upon this abuse of executive power; but notwithstanding it is seen that these favored convicts in most cases either return to their criminal practices, or fail to establish themselves as useful citizens, the evil, though diminishing the last five years, is so seriously affecting the peace and morals of society at large, as to call for something more effective than the mere expression of public opinion.

The restraining influence of penal justice is destroyed by the frequency of pardons. *The few,* of doubtful purposes and character, are thus benefitted at the cost of *the many,* and the best interests of the public. Laws, which are continually set aside, are derided; and sentences, continually reversed, bring the dignity and authority of the highest courts of justice into contempt. Let the *periods* of sentence, except for wilful murder, be shortened by the judges; but let them, unless in extreme cases, be served out.

In nearly all, of some hundred examples, which have come to my knowledge, the pardoned culprit has not become the upright citizen, and, in many cases, the lapse of a few months or weeks, or days even, finds the offender pursuing his accustomed career of vice and crime.

In twelve months, for the fiscal year ending November 1843,—of 460 convicts, 45 were pardoned out of the Ohio penitentiary. In the year, ending November, 1844, 50 convicts were pardoned out of the same prison; 49 by the executive, and 1 by the president of the United States.

In the Massachusetts prison, during the fiscal year, ending September, 1840, 14 prisoners of 322 were discharged by pardon, or remission of sentence. In the year, ending September, 1844, 15 were discharged by pardon and remission of sentence, and 4 by order of court.

In the Maine State prison, of 781 convicts received, from 1824 to 1842, 119 were pardoned.

In the Vermont State prison, in 1844, of 67 convicts, 11 were pardoned.

In the New Hampshire prison, in 1840, of 78 convicts 14 were pardoned; in 1841, of 84 convicts 7 were pardoned; in 1842, of 92 convicts 3 were pardoned; in 1843, of 89 convicts 15, according to official records, were pardoned.

In the Eastern and Western penitentiaries, in Pennsylvania, of an average of 508 convicts, 22 were pardoned in 1841; of 522 convicts, 39 were pardoned in 1842; of 522 prisoners, 31 were pardoned in 1843; and of 497 prisoners, 68 were pardoned in 1844. I ought to add that several of those released the past year were cases of peculiar hardship, from circumstances attending their conviction. But I have much reason to believe that, to the largest part, their own good and that of society would have been better consulted, by their detention till the expiration of their sentences.

In New Jersey the pardoning power is rarely exercised; never in Delaware; and seldom in Rhode Island. Prisoners for criminal offences, in the two last named States, are not many.

In Virginia, there were pardoned, from the penitentiary at Richmond, in 1839, 9 convicts; in 1840, 10; in 1841, 6; in 1842, 9; in 1843, 6; in all 40 for five years; the average of prisoners being, within a fraction, 189. In the five preceding years, the pardons were *thirty-five*, and the average about 161. Compared with the number of prisoners, and the duration of punishment with the length of the sentences, the number of pardoned from this prison is smaller than in most other states.

In Maryland, during the years 1841—'42—'43—'44, the pardons were 69; the average of convicts being 289 and a fraction.

The average of pardons in the state of New-York, from 1825 to 1835, was as 1 to 4; and within the last ten years 398 have been pardoned from the Auburn prison alone.

From the two penitentiaries in the State of New York, in 1842, there were pardoned 76 of 1523 convicts; and, in 1844, there were released by pardons 85 of 1713. The whole number of persons convicted, as recorded in the cities of New York, in 1842, were 1,336, embracing no returns from Rochester and Hudson. Of these, 702 were born in the United States; 423 in Ireland; 69 in England; 43 in Germany; and the rest in European countries and islands; 373 could neither read nor write; 147 could read, but not write; 608 could just read and write; the remaining 208 had received a tolerable common education, as official records show. Of the above, 802 were convicted in the city of New York. The same year, 1842, the whole number of convictions for *criminal* offences in the state was 1602, as returned by the clerks of the courts; but the number of persons convicted was but 1522, there being 80 convicted more than one time. Of these 1414 were men, and 108 were women. The whole number of convictions, in 1842, criminal cases and others, inclusive, were 2741; of these 2355 were men, and 386 were women, tried in the courts of record. Of the minor offences I have not the authorized returns.

In a large number of cases the pardoned convicts, in the States above referred to, gave no special evidence of reformation; but especially was this the case in New York and Pennsylvania; nor was there, with few exceptions, any thing in their moral, physical, or social condition, nor in their prospects of occupation when enlarged, nor were any mitigating circumstances adduced and proved in extenuation of their crimes, developed after trial and conviction, which should have recommended them to the gubernatorial clemency. It is well known that large numbers took advantage of their enlargement only to repeat transgressions; and many have been returned to the penitentiaries whence they were discharged, or been received into prisons in other States.

It can been shown that the most culpable offender has the fairest chance of escape from merited punishment; and it is a fact too well known, both in New York and Pennsylvania, to require proof by reference to official records, that convicts who are most dangerous to the peace and welfare of society have been enlarged. The pardons last year, granted to so large a number of prisoners in Pennsylvania, reached not the more deserving convicts, but those who of all beside should have been detained in restraint. The same was the case in many instances in New York. In some cases I know, as at Auburn, and several elsewhere, as shown in the reports and related to me by the officers, convicts in a low state of health, and considered by the physicians as past recovery, have been pardoned that they might receive the last offices of declining life from their friends and relatives. To this no humane person can object; and it may be remarked here that these facts reveal in part the insufficiency of the tables, which record the annual number of deaths, to indicate strictly the mortality in prisons; and as some writers upon these subjects seem to place an undue estimate upon tables, as showing physical as well as *moral* conditions, I have thought proper to allude to this fact. According to the Report of the Physician of the Auburn prison, there were, ' in 1843, *eleven* deaths, and *twelve* pardoned to save life!' This cannot have been usual, since I know that kind care is bestowed on the sick at all the prisons; and in most cases they have more judicious nursing and better medical care, than they would receive if discharged. But the majority of convicts, who are pardoned from all the prisons in this country, are in a good state of health. They are not, save in few instances, selected by or through the influence and recommendation of the officers, but by exertions of friends and associates abroad.

It is a very well established fact that, of late years, the most notorious offenders are amongst those who have had the advantage of the executive clemency, especially those sentenced for life for the highest crimes.

In the State of New York, in a period of ten years, sixty convicts, under sentence for life, received pardon, none having been imprisoned so long as seven years, several less than three or two years, and one less than ten months. It is seen that these prisoners, sentenced for life, really had advantage over those sentenced for ten, for seven, and for five years. In this working of the law, and use of the pardoning power, it clearly becomes the prisoners' interest to get the longest possible sentence.

I certainly would not altogether dispense with the pardoning power, but I believe that some restrictions on the Executive privilege would be a great public good, and regarded as such, even by those who now exercise unlimited power. If, as in Connecticut, the pardons could be granted but at one season in the year, and, in addition, if a special court, or council, could be created, associating with the governor, the senate, and two or more of the prison-inspectors, to inquire into the true merits of each case ; if these were to constitute a Court of Pardons, I am confident that much mischief, now resulting from the undue clemency of the executive, would cease ; and those only would be released for whom an urgent plea could be advanced, and who are peculiarly objects of this humane use of power and mercy.

DIET.—Diet in prisons is in general more carefully attended to than formerly. I have latterly observed no neglect at any prison at the time of my visits, nor any special wants, except at the Sing Sing prisons. These deficiencies may have been in part remedied, but the food can never be served comfortably, nor, as I think, decently, under present arrangements. Much unnecessary discomfort might be avoided by the construction of an eating-room arranged as at Auburn. It is quite impossible to serve food for more than 800 men in separate vessels, and distribute this, after its apportionment, the prisoners marching abroad, and to their cells to eat there, and have it in good condition. The kitchen department in prisons cannot be too closely inspected, both as to the quality and quantity of food prepared, the mode of preparing, and the distribution of it. The prisons at Auburn, Baltimore, and Wethersfield, offer, in the kitchen department, the best examples of any which are organized on the ' silent system,' unless the House of Correction at South Boston, is included, which is the best of all, in this, as in most other details.

Diet in the prisons under the separate system, receives a very commendable degree of attention. Articles of good quality, wholesome food, and well prepared, may be depended on through the care of the superior officers.

Dr. Hartshorne, late resident physician of the Eastern Penitentiary, offers the following remarks in his report to the Legislature, for 1844.

" Much is due, to circumspection exercised in the regulation of the diet generally, and in particular cases, as well as to a more intelligent attention paid to the proper physical condition of the inmates, in regard to temperature, cleanliness, exercise, and suitable employment.

The diet of the prison is decidedly a full one, and as the convicts are in general eager for the largest rations, their keepers can allow them, more mischief must be apprehended from excess than from any other fault. Accordingly, a greater restriction in the daily allowance of meat and soup has been found advisable during the oppressive heat of summer. Mutton, with its mild broth, and bacon without any, alternate successively with the ordinary fresh beef, the soup of which is rendered more nutritious, by the free addition of okra, rice, and other mucilaginous vegetables. The breakfast of bread and coffee remains unchanged, but at night, tea, cocoa, or weak coffee, with a small ration of bread, are substituted for the Indian-meal porridge and molasses, which make their supper during three-fourths of the year. The cultivated grounds between the blocks and round the main wall produce ample supplies of a variety of green vegetables, which are liberally furnished, with the potatoes or rice, in the daily dinner mess. Large quantities of tomatoes, onions, lettuce, and cabbage, are distributed uncooked from time to time among the men, and with the vinegar, salt and pepper for every cell, afford refreshing salads, which, to say the least, must abundantly protect the prisoner from the inroads of the scurvy. Vegetables of this description, as well as flowers, are also cultivated by many of the convicts themselves in their airing

5

yards, and are thus made the instruments of productive and very interesting amusements."

WATER.—At most of the prisons on the Auburn plan, the supply of water is inadequate to the wants of the prisoners, and for all general purposes. In summer, at Charlestown, Baltimore, and elsewhere, it is procured by transportation. These deficiencies are shortly to be remedied by the construction of tanks or cisterns. No prisons are so abundantly supplied with water as those of Pennsylvania; none so miserably and uniformly bad from the beginning till now, as the Sing Sing prisons. 'During the month of September, the expense of supplying these prisons with water, *and that very scantily, was about $10 per day.*' These prisons have never, at any period, had *pure* water; never a sufficient supply for cooking and washing; and as for personal ablutions, I must pass by the special practices and the wants together. At some seasons, and under favorable circumstances, a part of the men-convicts have been allowed to bathe in the river.* Measures are in progress to secure this absolutely imperative demand for these prisons. To the deficiency, I think, may be referred much of the sickness which has at times prevailed here.

Great attention is paid to personal cleanliness in the prison at Wethersfield.

The prisoners and prison at Washington, D. C., exhibit care throughout in this respect.

In the Rhode Island prison, the inspectors decided (Sept. 1844) according to printed rules and regulations, that 'the convicts in good health may be allowed the privilege of the warm bath *once in three months!* Cold water is supplied daily.

In Charlestown, the accommodations for bathing are limited to an occasional plunge (sometimes once a week) into a collection of water, called the canal, or canal lock†—within the yard, and exposed to the weather; of course, a large portion of the year, but little resorted to. The prisoners wash face and hands

---

* Tide water reaches above Mount Pleasant, rendering the water of the river unfit for cooking, the use of the laundry, &c.

† Till recently this lock has been the outlet of the sewers and drains from the prison and offices.

in the shops; all the prisons, constructed on the Auburn plan, are deficient in arrangements for proper and sufficient washing and bathing; and it is known that no water is carried to the cells, except for drinking, and this in small measures, thus precluding the possibility of washing there. In all the prisons constructed on the Pennsylvania plan, the water being conveyed through iron pipes into each apartment, the prisoners have every facility for personal cleanliness; and I am glad to say, that this is enjoined both in the County as well as in the State prisons. In the Eastern Penitentiary, in addition to cold-water bathing in the cell-rooms, which are comfortable both in summer and winter, and convenient, each being furnished ' with a tub, a wash-basin, soap, and towels,' the convicts have the warm bath once a week—the women in a commodious room adjacent to their gallery, and the men in bath-rooms constructed at the end of one of the corridors. Mr. Thompson, the judicious and competent warden, regarding personal cleanliness important, in its moral as well as physical influences, spares no care to secure this, and the means of preserving it, to every prisoner.

" The mode adopted is attended with very little expense, and is as follows :—the daily escape-steam from the engine, is passed into a tank containing about 80 hogsheads of water, which thereby is maintained at a temperature of about 90° ; ten separate cells, each having a bath, receive the prisoners, that are brought separately by their overseers, and are allowed fifteen minutes for bathing; soap, fresh supplies of water, and dry towels, being furnished for each. By this means, 40 can bathe per hour, without any infringement of the separate system, —an officer walking in front of the grated doors of the bathing cells, effectually preventing any possibility of communication."

Another arrangement, which in most prisons is sadly too much overlooked, is care in airing the beds and bed-clothing. I ought to say that there is no omission of this sort in the prison at Wethersfield ; and wish I could, with truth, add the same commendation of all other prisons on the Auburn plan. The extremely small lodging cells of these, call for special care in this respect. Too much attention cannot be paid to cleanliness in prisons,

CLOTHING.—In all the prisons on the ' separate plan,' clothing is suitable and appropriate for the seasons. The apparel in prisons on the ' silent or Auburn system' is, with occasional exceptions, sufficient and comfortable at all seasons, except in the men's prison at Sing Sing. And I cannot but think, that, when the physician, in his report for 1844, remarking on the great amount and severity of autumnal sickness, ascribes this ' to sudden change of temperature,' he might have added, as collateral causes, the use of bad water, and insufficient supplies of water for all purposes, and the want of suitable clothing to meet the necessity occasioned by sudden access of cold weather. The inspectors report ' 214 of the convicts in the men's prison under treatment at one time ;' the physician states ' the average of sick for the month, of 868 men, 101.4-30 (?) daily prescribed for.'

The diseases recorded in the cold months are ' colds, coughs, rheumatic complaints, and consumption ;—in August and September, remittent and typhoid fevers, cholera morbus and diarrhœa.' I cannot learn from the tabular records the number of individual cases of sickness ; the monthly average being given of cases in the hospitals, and cases prescribed for in mass, and in whole numbers and *fractions !*

The resident physician at the Eastern Penitentiary, Dr. Given, refers to the health and hygienic regulations in that Institution as follows :

" As might have been expected, the greatest number of prisoners on the sick-list at one time, occurred in the months of July and August. The diseases most frequent at that period were those incident to the season,—diarrhœa and dysentery ; and of these (from information furnished me by physicians practising in the neighbourhood,) I have reason to believe we were far from having our due proportion, either in extent or severity. This comparative freedom from bowel complaints during the summer, I believe to be solely attributable to the Warden having substituted tea and coffee in the evening in place of mush ; and for dinner mutton and mutton-soup in lieu of beef and vegetables, which constitute the ordinary prison diet.

" Though encircled during the autumn by severe endemic remittent and intermittent fevers, not a single case of either occurred within the walls of the Institution.

" Rheumatism, heretofore a very prominent item in the sick-list, is now comparatively unknown to us ; owing, no doubt, to the full supply of flannel under-clothes furnished each prisoner, as well as the great care and attention given by the Warden to the proper heating of the cells.

" The weekly use, by each prisoner, of the warm-baths, now in operation, will, I am certain, contribute still farther to the general health of the Institution."

It should not be forgotten in stating apparent special causes of sickness in prisons, that with few exceptions, the convicts arrive at them with constitutions broken and health impaired by irregular modes of life and vicious habits : and so many causes may affect health, and lead to confirmed disease and death, that tables recording these in any prisons, cannot be made use of with any sort of assurance, in deducing the comparative health of one prison over another, or the respective counts of mortality. Neither the ' *separate* system' nor the ' *silent* system' conduct necessarily in their administration, to disease and death, the usual rules of health being attended to; but it is as great a folly to expect exemption from these in any or all prisons, as it is to abuse one prison or commend another, because a few more die in one at one time than another. Differences of climate, differences of constitution, as of blacks and whites ; a thousand considerations render it as difficult as it is preposterous to compare the health of the prisons in our country with each other, even under the ordinary circumstances of good government in all. The wonder is, that there is so little sickness in prisons, when the history of the prisoners is remembered—and that there is not more, must be ascribed to the advantage of *regular hours* of working, eating, and sleeping, and restraint from bad habits.

VENTILATION.—The ventilation of prisons, though not overlooked is insufficiently provided for. This subject fails to receive the imperative attention it demands. Lodging cells on the Auburn plan, though often whitewashed, and aired by day, become almost insufferably impure during the evening, and by night. The occupants of the upper and lower ranges of cells from varying and opposite causes, have appeared to me to suffer most. The most destructive, and ever-present impurity in prison cells, is carbonic acid gas. Continuance in atmospheres increasingly and excessively charged with carbonic acid gas, enervates both the mind and the body, induces heaviness and

stupor, and diminishes the appetite. Feeble constitutions soonest sink under these depressing influences. I am satisfied that the want of pure air, of proper temperature, is the occasion of most of the feebleness at times observed in prisons and elsewhere. Let none judge of what these are by night, or of the state of air in the areas by night, from the freer ventilation secured by day, when the cells are vacated. Go after the convicts have been locked up for two or three hours, and traverse, if you can, the galleries and areas, and the defects of *all* these prisons, in respect to ventilation, will be revealed in a way not to be forgotten. The mode of warming these prisons, destroys the life-influence of the air. The iron stoves in the areas, in which fires are maintained, keeping the iron at a red heat, partially deoxygenize the air; carbonic acid gas accumulates, and combining with gross animal exhalations, fill the spaces in the prisons and cells, and there remain for want of sufficient currents of pure air to carry off these impurities. The insufficient supply of pure air from abroad, to keep up the quantity of oxygen consumed by respiration, with other causes, conduces to much feebleness and disease. The warden of the prison at Auburn, anxious to remedy these mischiefs, lately employed pulverized gypsum in the cells and areas; but there is nothing in this substance to recommend it as a valuable disinfector. Common lime, chemically considered, is better, merely applied frequently as a wash. This is constantly and freely employed at Auburn, but does not secure a pure state of air: and nothing can, in those vast ranges of small occupied cells, except continual strong currents from abroad, and wide ventilators within.*
Chloride of lime is sometimes resorted to, but this after standing a little time, forms a crust, and, if undisturbed, is no longer an active purifying agent; beside, if evolved in large quantities, in small occupied apartments which are imperfectly ventilated, it is highly deleterious, being one of the most irritating of

---

* Atmospheric air freely introduced by good ventilation, must always be considered the most important of all fumigations for ordinary purposes, and a material, which is, in general, sufficient to oxydate or burn off, by slow combustion, innumerable impurities that are apt to be developed in stagnant atmospheres, particularly where animal and vegetable matters abound, though for extreme cases, it has not the power and energy of lime, chlorine, or acids.—REID ON VENTILATION,

all the gases, and also tending to corrode and destroy metallic substances. *Nitric acid* is an active disinfecting agent and absorbent, and may be employed when the use of any.foreign substance is judged absolutely necessary. Cleanliness is better than the introduction of any of these agents, and I cannot forbear again referring to the House of Correction at South Boston, for an illustration of this fact.

HEAT.—There is difficulty in procuring in winter, an *equal* and sufficient distribution of *heat* in the prisons on the Auburn plan. I know of no prison where, as yet, the officers express themselves fully satisfied with the use of the area stoves to procure a good supply of heat in the cold months. In the mild season fires are kept up to dry the prisons, and to promote ventilation ; and, as the doors and windows are open during the day, a comfortable and tolerably equal temperature is preserved. This fails in the winter ; some cells being hot and stifling, others cold and uncomfortable.

Most prisons on the Pennsylvania plan, are heated by means of iron tubes containing hot water or steam ; as yet, at some of the prisons, there is difficulty in *equalizing* the temperature throughout all parts of the prison during the coldest season. The Pentonville prison, near London, appears to have secured the most perfect heating apparatus, and it is to be hoped that this plan may be adopted in American prisons, now building or to be constructed. The Moyamensing prison is heated with hot air.

The prisoner has a right to share in prison, comfortable clothing, wholesome food, pure air, and a free use of water, equally with a humane discipline and ample means of moral instruction. Government, securing these, may claim and expect in return diligence, subordination, and rigid compliance with the rules of the prison, with submission to its necessary restraints and efforts to improve.

HEALTH.—The health of prisons is a very important subject of consideration, and the examination of tables exhibited in the several annual reports, from the mixed methods of presenting them, are of difficult comparison ; even were this not the case, no close deductions I apprehend, *can be* derived from them, and no general comparative conclusions can be drawn for less periods than 5 or 10 years. The number of deaths in the Connecticut prison last year was unusually large, but it would be absurd to charge the *system* with this result. The deaths in the State prison at Charlestown, have the past year been unusually few, and there are but few patients in the Infirmary, but the prisoners do not by any means appear in as good health as those in the house of Correction at South Boston, or the prisons at Wethersfield, and at Trenton.

After visiting large prisons in, or adjacent to, cities, I have the habit of visiting also those districts where the same trades are carried on by men at liberty : especially have I carried out this comparison in Philadelphia in the weaving districts, and at different seasons of the year. In New York, Massachusetts, Pennsylvania, New Jersey, Maryland and Virginia, I find the prisoners in as good physical condition in prisons, as are men working at the same trades at large, comparing individuals by fifties and hundreds, employed in weaving, spooling, shoe-making, iron-working, cabinet-making, tailoring, &c. I have seldom included those prisoners recently admitted, as the health *usually improves* by regular habits and diet, with equal hours of rest and labor. But let it be remembered, that house and shop-laborers, at liberty, and laborers in prison, alike suffer essentially and certainly for want of effectual, free ventilation in their work-rooms and lodging apartments.

A proper attention to ventilation of lodging-rooms, would much diminish the vice of intemperance, since it would remove some of its frequent exciting causes, feebleness, headache, and a sense of exhaustion.

The propriety of employing a resident physician, as is done in the Eastern Penitentiary, is recommended by the claims of humanity and the results of experience. In the most populous prisons especially, we have numerous examples of misery and serious injuries which might have been prevented by consulting *deliberately*, a competent medical attendant. An insane convict, with others, was a year or two since removed from one prison to another for more convenient division of numbers. The officer whose duty it was to report the case of insanity to the

Warden of the other prison, *forgot it;* the insane man refused to work, was accused of obstinacy, and repeatedly flogged till his shrieks and tortures compelled his ignorant and hard-judging officers to suspend the horrid punishment. He was removed to a hospital for the insane. An officer in another of the most approved prisons on the Auburn plan, testifies that a prisoner was committed, who declared himself unable to work. The officer believing him to be *obstinate,* flogged him repeatedly, (as the rules of the prison required,) but fearing he might be wrong, the Warden was summoned, who considered it a case of mere deception. The flogging was repeated very severely in the afternoon ; the following morning the man was found dead in his bed. The post-mortem examination discovered extensive disease! Had there been a resident physician present, or had the responsible physician been called, what misery might have been spared. While I would speak respectfully of the ability of Physicians who attend at most of the prisons, I must express the opinion that often too little time is spent in examining the physical and mental condition of the convicts.

The Insane in Prisons.—From the Massachusetts State prison ' 7 insane convicts are reported to have been transferred to the State Hospital, during the year ending September, 1844.' In the Connecticut state prison, July 1844, ' 2 only are represented as wholly insane, and 4 partially; all being so at the time of commitment.' ' No provision,' writes the physician, 'is made for sending an insane convict to the Hospital at Hartford.'

Inquiring at the prison at Auburn, concerning the *insane,* I found, that having no authority to send their patients to the State Hospital, they have conveyed them to the Bloomingdale Asylum, when so violent as to require much active care. The quiet patients are employed in the shops. One poor fellow, who had served out his time, and was but a degree above idiocy, was discharged the day I was last at the prison ; the officers appeared to commiserate his friendlessness and incapacity to take care of himself, and took much pains, after clothing him comfortably, and giving him some money, to make him understand its value and use. He was no subject for convict discipline, and the Warden assured me never had been.

Of the insane in the prison at Sing Sing, one of the Inspectors writes to me as follows :—

" Aug. 28, 1844. As to the insane, it is difficult to give you any satisfactory answer. The line of demarkation between the sane and the insane is not easily defined. We are making a thorough investigation on this subject. We are not authorized to send any of our prisoners to the State Hospital for the Insane at Utica. We are therefore now erecting an out-ward for the treatment of the insane upon the plan pursued in our best regulated asylums. At present the provision for them is exceedingly imperfect."

A deplorable necessity that, which urges the construction of a hospital within the boundaries of a prison.

In November 1844, the committee reported, that beside four insane sent to Bloomingdale, 31 of the 868 convicts were insane. Most of these were insane when committed. Insanity is sometimes developed in this, as in all other prisons, but so also is it in communities; and I consider neither the ' silent' nor ' separate' systems as specially disposing convicts to insanity; but the want of pure air in the lodging-cells is, I doubt not, one of the many exciting causes of this malady in all prisons, and in all institutions in which ventilation is defective.

In the Eastern Penitentiary, during 1844, twelve convicts were admitted in a state of insanity. Within two years, *twenty-seven* have been received in that condition, charged with various crimes. These were entered as insane by the sheriffs who delivered them to the custody of the warden, and known to be so at such times, and long previous.

In February last, I saw six insane convicts in the prison at Trenton, all of whom I ascertained to have been committed in that condition. From this prison, as from the Eastern Penitentiary, I traced the history of these convicts to the several counties, whence they were committed, in order to assure myself of the absolute fact of insanity *previous* to their committal.

In the Western Penitentiary, August, 1844, I found but *one* absolutely insane convict; three were simple, or of very weak understanding. A letter from the chaplain of this prison contains the following reference to this subject.

" I have given the subject particular and close attention, only for a short time ; but, in the period of my labors here, I am ready to testify, that the ' separate' system has no more tendency to produce insanity than any other form of imprisonment. The *mild influence* which soothes the convict in his separate cell ; the frequent presence of the officers, who carry his food, instruct him in his employments, receive his work ; together with the aids of the moral instructor, the visits of the physician, the warden, and inspectors, and the use of books, unite to maintain an equable state of mind."

In the prison at Columbus, I saw two decidedly insane ; in the prison at Baltimore, the same month, *three*, but not excited. In the prison at Richmond, *two ;* the persons of these, and the cells, all indicated care on the part of the several officers in charge. Great, very great inconvenience is experienced from this unhappy class of prisoners in all prisons ; they cannot receive from the prison-officers that appropriate and peculiar care their condition demands.

VISITORS.—Visitors' fees at Auburn, in 1842, were $1692.75, and, in 1845, $1942.75,—making $3635.50 ; at 25 cents each, we have for two years, at one prison, of paying visitors alone, 14542 persons. At Sing Sing, of paying visitors, was received, in 1843, $311.75, and in 1844, $236.62, making $548.37 ; (children half price) 2194 visitors, counting only one at $12\frac{1}{2}$ cents. Income from visitors for two years at Charlestown, $1487.75 ; allowing 25 cents for each paying visitor, there were admitted 5951 persons. At Wethersfield, the visitors' fees amounted in the last two years to $548.12\frac{1}{2}$, allowing 25 cents each, there were admitted 2192, allowing but one at half price ; but, if the fees are less than 25 cents, as is sometimes the custom, the number is greatly larger. At the prison in Windsor there were in one year 796 visitors, and during the same period in New Hampshire about 500 paying visitors, allowing 25 cents, more if a smaller sum. In Columbus, Ohio, in one year, 1844, was received $1038.78 for paying visitors, admitting, if we allow all to have been adults at full price, at 25 cents each, above 4150 persons. It might be supposed that the exposure of the convicts to such larger numbers of spectators, would not aid the moral and reforming influences of the prisons. This source of revenue would be better dispensed with.

DIMENSIONS OF LODGING CELLS, &C. IN THE STATE PENITENTIA-
RIES.

Maine.—Prison at Thomaston. The cells in use at the time of my last visit are now abandoned. The new prison, then in progress of erection, I have not seen since it was completed.

New-Hampshire.—Prison at Concord. Cells in the new prison 6 feet 10 inches long; 3 feet 4 inches wide; 6 feet 4 inches high. Ventilation defective; tobacco freely used. *Meals taken in these cells!* Area, between the cell walls and the outer walls, but 8 feet wide. Three tiers of cells.

Vermont.—Prison at Windsor. Cells 7 feet long; 3 feet 6 inches wide; 6 feet 9 inches high. Ventilated through the door and ceiling insufficiently; the use of tobacco allowed, somewhat in less excess than in New-Hampshire. *Meals taken in the cells.* Area 11 feet wide, ventilated but insufficiently, by windows in the outer walls.

Connecticut.—Prison at Wethersfield. Cells 7 feet by 3 feet 6 inches, and 7 feet high. Broad area, well ventilated. Meals taken in the cells. This is the most accurately neat and thoroughly clean prison in the United States. I have never found it neglected. Every thing is in order. Cells in four stories.

Massachusetts.—Prison at Charlestown. Cells 7 feet by 3½ feet, and 7 feet high; very deficient ventilation. Meals are taken in the cells, thereby increasing the difficulties of maintaining cleanliness and pure air. This prison now, August, 1845, compares, in respect to the general appearance of the prisoners, cell-habits, and other arrangements, disadvantageously with the penitentiaries in Connecticut and Maryland, which I have also lately visited. The beds, bed-clothing, &c., are this year in bad condition, revealing *animated*, as well as other sources of offence.

Rhode-Island.—Prison at Providence. Cells 15 feet by 8 feet, and 8 feet high on the lower story; on the second, they are about 3 feet less in length, but, being higher, contain about the same number of cubic feet. The cells are kept clean, and in all respects suitably furnished. Prison neat and well ordered; the county jail, (which is connected with it,) is, on the

45

other hand, *very bad indeed.* The keeper has repeatedly urged important alterations ; as yet without effect.

New-York.—State prisons are at Auburn, Sing Sing, and one now in progress of building in the *mining* district, in Clinton county, 14 miles west of Plattsburg! The penitentiary at Auburn contains 770 sleeping cells; these are $7\frac{1}{2}$ feet long, 3 feet 8 inches wide, and 7 feet high. They are raised upon five stories. The area is lighted by large windows opening through the outer wall, and is nine feet wide from floor to roof. The ventilation, notwithstanding all these flues and windows, is intolerably bad. Great care is taken to preserve general cleanliness, and much is gained by the prisoners taking their meals in a large well-arranged apartment, where their food is decently served, as at the Maryland penitentiary in Baltimore, and that at Washington, D. C. Except in prisons established on the ' separate' system, where the cells are all of large size, this arrangement for the prisoners is demanded alike by decency and justice. The present warden pays uncommon attention to secure supplies of wholesome food ; especially inspecting the quality of the beef, pork and flour, consumed here. At one time much ill health was produced by a culpable indifference to the quality of the kitchen supplies.

The men's prison on Mount Pleasant, at Sing Sing, contains 1000 lodging cells, constructed in tiers of two ranges on a story, back to back, surrounded by an area nine feet wide, lighted by windows through a wall three feet in thickness ; each cell is 7 feet long, 7 feet high, and $3\frac{1}{2}$ feet wide. The ventilation is altogether insufficient, and all the cells compare disadvantageously with those I examined in Connecticut and Virginia. The situation of this prison renders the cells damp, even fires in the stoves fail to correct this disadvantage. The cells, except a few, are not clean ; and I am not sure that they can, under existing circumstances, be maintained in what I should call the best order. The highest tiers are not in the best condition.

New Jersey Penitentiary* at South Trenton, is constructed

* The New Jersey Penitentiary, as well as the two Penitentiaries in Pennsylvania, and several county prisons, were constructed under the direction of Haviland, who is so well known for his architectural abilities.

on the *separate* plan, with radiating wings or blocks. The corridors are 14 feet wide, the cells are ranged on either side in two tiers, and are well lighted, but only tolerably ventilated; these cells are 12 feet by 8 in the clear. They are furnished with all needful accommodations, and have each an ample supply of water; this last is a means of promoting physical and mental health, not generally possessed in prisons, and is unfortunately too deficient in most of our public institutions.

Delaware has no Penitentiary; the common jail at Newcastle is kept clean, but the prisoners, waiting trial, and after sentence, are associated in common. At the time of my visit, in May, 1845, I found the apartments filled with offenders of various ages and degrees in crime, whose mutually corrupting influence, as in almost every jail in the United States, qualified them for greater misdeeds in future. Punishment usually speedily follows conviction in Delaware : the law is inexorable, and there is no appeal from the whipping-post and the pillory. Conversation with several eminent jurists and citizens in public life in Delaware, revealed their opinion as altogether in *favor* of this mode of administering justice; some strong arguments were adduced in favor of the system, as the rare occurrence of second convictions; but, granting its efficacy as a terror to evil-doers, it is difficult to concede any thing beside. I cannot conceive that the use of the lash can fail to render a hardened offender yet more callous to public opinion, and a brutal man more brutalized and brutalizing in his habits. The same offenders will not perhaps quickly repeat transgressions in the same neighbourhood, but, as a general rule, they will not be reformed in life, nor aided in reform; they may be restrained, but they are not radically better men. The argument of less crime in Delaware than in adjacent States is no evidence of the greater excellence of the penal code, and superior efficacy of the lash and pillory, over imprisonment under the *silent* system on the one hand, or the *separate* system on the other. Delaware, in fact, offers less temptation to crime, and fewer facilities for escape from its penalties, than either Pennsylvania or Maryland, and I conceive this to be the true ground of greater exemption from criminal offences in proportion to the population of this state, than in others adjacent or remote. Since 1829, there have been committed to the Eastern Penitentiary of Pennsylvania, 118 criminals, natives of the little State of Delaware.

Pennsylvania.—The Western Penitentiary in Alleghany city is built on the radiating plan, the cells ranging on either side of corridors running down the centre of the buildings, twelve feet in width. The cells are 15 feet long by 8 wide; are well lighted, and tolerably ventilated. They are well furnished, and abundantly supplied with water.

The Eastern Penitentiary, at Philadelphia, is built on the radiating plan, and consists of a central building, from which radiate seven wings or blocks. Three of these wings contain each 38 cells, the other four, 472 cells. The upper story of the last built blocks contains a series of two apartments, opening into one, as a compensation for the want of an exercise yard, or access to the wider grounds. A part of the cells on the ground floor are 11 feet 9 inches by 7 feet 6 inches, arched at top, and 16 feet 6 inches to the highest part of the ceiling. In the four last built blocks, the cells on the ground floor are nearly 16 feet in length, affording convenient space for the looms, and other furniture. These large cells, or more strictly apartments, are well lighted and ventilated. They have a constant supply of pure water, and are furnished with all needful accommodations. The prisoners of course eat in their respective rooms.

Maryland Penitentiary in Baltimore, contains in the eastern wing, 320 cells for the male convicts, which range against the outer wall instead of being thrown into the centre. I greatly prefer this arrangement, affording as it does advantages of light and air, unknown in ranges of centre cells, so inconvenient and tomb-like in construction as those all are. The two ranges, which have five stories each, are divided by a passage fifteen feet wide, in which stoves are placed, and fires maintained to dissipate occasional dampness, and to promote ventilation. The prisoners eat in common, and are served with wholesome food.

District of Columbia.—Penitentiary at Washington. The men's prison is 120 feet long by 50 wide, and 36 feet high.

The cells are on the Auburn plan, and are 7 feet 11 inches by 3 feet 4 inches, and 7 feet 9 inches high. The windows in the outer wall are large, and the area is 12 feet 3 inches wide. The ventilation here is more free than in the New York prisons, but is far from perfect. I found the cells clean and decently furnished, and remarked a generally neat appearance in the eating hall.

The wing appropriated to the women was clean, but the occupants, having no matron, were neither distinguished for silence nor industry.

Ohio Penitentiary is at Columbus, and planned to receive 700 sleeping cells in the men's prison; these are constructed on the Auburn plan, back to back, ranged in five stories, and have an area rather more than 11 feet wide. Here fires in large stoves are kept up through the year, to absorb the dampness, and to promote a freer circulation of air. The prisoners eat in a spacious hall, which is kept clean; supply of food ample, and sufficiently varied. Of 438, (450, including the women's department, and several convicts newly admitted on the 20th,) but 8 were on the sick list, and this during a season when much indisposition prevails generally in the country. Each wing contains 70 cells on each story; these are 7 feet by 3 feet 6 inches, and 7 feet high. The ventilation is exceedingly defective. There was no matron in the women's wing at the time I was there, the 19th and 20th of August, 1844, and they were not slow to exercise their good and evil gifts on each other.

Virginia.—Penitentiary at Richmond. The dimensions of the cells are 12 feet by 6 feet 6 inches wide, and 9 feet high, the ceiling being arched. These are lighted and ventilated, but not warmed in winter. I cannot, in that mild climate, regard this as a serious evil, since the convicts pass the days in the work shops. The prisoners eat in their cells; the size of these renders this custom less objectionable than in prisons constructed more exactly on the Auburn plan. The use of tobacco is allowed.

MORAL, RELIGIOUS, AND GENERAL INSTRUCTION IN PRISONS.

This subject, so important and so intimately associated with the idea of reformation for the convict, has, with rare exceptions, in most States, heretofore received a consideration quite inadequate to its bearing on the welfare of society, and the purposes which modern prison systems have professed to urge as of primary necessity.

In the prison at Thomaston, Maine, a chaplain, appointed by law, attends as required. No system of general instruction is adopted. The inspectors, concluding their report for 1842, remark, that ' The law requires the chaplain, in addition to his services on the Sabbath, to make daily visits to the prison, for the purpose of conversing with the convicts:' and add, that ' the effect of such visits is to afford opportunity for such as are inclined, to spend a part of their time in idleness and deception, while their sentence requires constant labour !'

There are two services on Sunday, and a Bible class or Sunday School was established in the hope that it would produce good results. The chaplain reports, that ' The number is not large who will voluntarily attend this, and we consider it useless to compel them.' There are no regularly appointed visitors at this prison, of experience and ability, to instruct the prisoners, and the labors of the chaplain appear to be chiefly confined to special religious duties. The prison is deficient in a supply of books, and the means of general moral instruction, as well as instruction on the subjects of common education.

In the prison at Concord, New Hampshire, those of the convicts, who cannot read and write, are taught by the chaplain, who is appointed by law, and who is interested in advancing the well-being of those under restraint. There are two services on Sunday, the order of exercises being the same as in the churches abroad. The largest part of the day, not so occupied, is spent by the chaplain in going from cell to cell, conversing with and teaching the prisoners. It will be perceived that other aid is needed. There were 89 convicts in 1844, evidently a larger number, when the hours for teaching are considered, than one person can attend to. There is a small library, and each prisoner is furnished with a weekly temperance paper, and a religious paper. The chaplain remarks in a report for 1844, that the 'largest proportion of the convicts were destitute of early moral culture, and religious instruction. Some, from their earliest childhood, have been exposed to the worst examples,' 'and more than half have committed crimes under the influence of intemperance.'

"A few have fallen victims to the cunning of more sagacious offenders ; but the truth is irresistible, that, *in most instances, the want of early* moral culture, and the use of intoxicating drinks, have more effect than all causes beside in bringing the convict to his low condition."

Increased attention is given to instruction in this prison, and it is hoped that judicious measures will be adopted to advance this important work. I think the custom of admitting citizens generally, to the chapel services on Sunday, should be discontinued, as unsuitable in all respects ; at once exposing the prisoners to improper observation, and necessarily distracting their attention from the duties of the time and place.

The prison at Windsor, Vermont, has a chaplain appointed by law, who holds two services on every Sunday, and attends prayers at the close of each day ; he also visits the prisoners in their cells, and in the shops, 'from time to time.' I remarked that the officers were disposed to sustain moral influences, and the warden, judging from his conversation, had the good of the prisoners at heart. But here, as in other prisons already mentioned, the means for careful and sufficient instruction of the convicts are too little considered, and the importance of this too little regarded by government. The hours of teaching and learning are chiefly confined to a portion of the Sabbath.

The State prison of Connecticut, at Wethersfield, has a chaplain, who according to the statute, is required to spend his whole time in the instruction of the prisoners. He holds service on Sunday, and the convicts are assembled morning and evening for prayers. The Sunday school is taught by the officers of the prison ; those of the convicts attend who are under

25 years of age, and are divided into Bible and Reading classes.

The chaplain, a religious and intelligent man, who is zealous in his work, appeals as follows to the Directors, in behalf of the convicts :—

"I submit to the directors, with great respect, and yet with earnestness, in behalf of my unhappy charge, whether the letter or the spirit of this benign law," referring to the statute, "can be executed, or the benevolent intentions of the Legislature carried out fully, under a system which has for its great object the mere making of money, and under which little instruction can be communicated, except at seasons when the men are so fatigued that they cannot be excited to mental effort?"

The chaplain proceeds to suggest a plan which proposes dividing the men prisoners into six classes, two, at different times for each working day of the week, which he proposes to instruct for an hour each, thus securing two hours a week for regular moral, and general educational teaching.

"In this manner," he continues, "new trains of thought might be suggested, new mental efforts aroused, and the mind, long debased by ignorance, indulgence, and crime, may be awakened to hope and amendment, to sentiments of affection and self-respect."

These views were also strongly urged by the predecessors of the present chaplain. This care to lessen the severity of labor, in order to educate the conscience and the intellect, is alone needed to place the Connecticut prison on the best possible foundation for the 'silent system.' At present it affords the best example of that system in the United States, not being, like Auburn prison, crowded to excess, and in consequence possessing advantages for more correct, moral discipline. For many years however, in Connecticut, it has been the aim, not merely to make the prison support itself, which all prisons should do, but to render convict labor, and the *exhibition* of the *convicts*, a source of revenue to the State. This last mistaken custom is found in all the prisons of the northern States, and conducts to frequent and improper exposure of the convicts to the gaze and remarks of the curious and the inconsiderate.

Massachusetts State prison, at Charlestown, has a chaplain

appointed by law, who, like the other officers, is paid by the State. He holds one service on Sunday. 'Eight months of the year there is a Sunday school, before the service, at which those convicts who are interested, attend.' Those, who cannot read are formed into spelling classes and taught, others are instructed according to the views of those who are teachers. Singing, which is well conducted, makes a part of every service. Prayers are engaged in daily, morning and evening. The area, during the cold season, is lighted, in order that those prisoners, who wish, may read after being shut into their cells at night. I think that the lighting of all the cells cannot be done effectually; but, not having been there at evening, do not speak confidently. The chaplain writes for the convicts, when they wish to communicate with their friends: this office, though cheerfully performed, involves much labor, and I think consumes time that might be better employed in the instruction of the convicts, on the improved but limited plan proposed by the chaplain of the Wethersfield prison.

I see no reason why those prisoners who can write should not do so, accounting to the officer for the proper use of the writing materials, and submitting their letters to the Warden or Chaplain, as the law in other prisons enjoins. If the prisoner can see to read in his cell, he of course can see to write there. The chaplain remarks, in the annual report for 1844:

" The government of this commonwealth has wisely and benevolently *made provision for the employment of all requisite moral and religious* means and influences, on which principally reliance is to be placed for the moral improvement and reformation of the inmates of this institution."

On the same page, I read as follows:—

" The undersigned *is far from supposing that all the moral means and appliances* for the improvoment of *the prisoners is placed in his hands,*" &c.

In the latter sentiment I heartily concur,—and I conceive that, without breach of even as close discipline as that at Wethersfield, much less that at Charlestown, the moral, religious, and mental culture of the prisoners might be more effectually promoted. In addition to the cares of the chaplain, the convicts are furnished with temperance papers; some religious papers are also put into their hands, and tracts are circulated. Several hundred volumes of books are in circulation, which have been presented by individuals, from time to time, purchased, first by the sum of *fifty dollars* ' sent by the mother of a life-prisoner to her son, to furnish him with proper reading.' The books purchased with this sum he used for a time, and then put into general circulation, that his fellow-prisoners might be benefitted thereby!

Additions to the Library for several years past, have been made by the prisoners themselves, who on receiving their enlargement have often left the books which they brought when they were committed, or which had at a later period been supplied by their friends. A donation of *fifty* dollars was opportunely sent from New York, by persons friendly to this important means of promoting good in prisons; the sum was expended as designed by the donors. At the last session of the Legislature, $100 was appropriated to increase the number and variety of works already in use.

Rhode Island State prison at Providence, has no chaplain appointed or supported by the State. Mr. Douglas, the faithful home missionary of a Baptist society, in a general report of his labors, remarks,—

" I have repeatedly visited the county jail and State prison, but not so frequently as in former years; but little good can be accomplished for the prisoners in the jail, so long as they are without classification, and without employment; and I feel it to be the duty of the State to furnish moral and religious instruction to its convicts."

An act, passed in Rhode Island, in 1838, for establishing the discipline of the prison, contains the following section :—

5. " Instruction. Any person or persons licensed by the inspectors, *shall be allowed* as free intercourse with the convicts, for the purpose of giving them moral and religious instruction, as is consistent with the safe custody of the convicts. Public religious exercises may be held by such person in the corridor of said prison on the first day of the week, measures being taken to prevent the convicts during this time from seeing each other, or holding any communication with any one not authorised by the rules of the prison. Each cell shall be furnished with a Bible at the expense of the State, and one hour in each day shall be allowed each convict for perusal of the same, if he please."

Since the ' silent and congregated system' has been adopted, in place of the ' separate' plan,' (which here was never applied according to the Pennsylvania system, and, *as carried out here*, was wisely discontinued,) the religious service on Sunday is attended in the large work-room, which is commodious and exceedingly comfortable. The very small number of prisoners, there seldom being twenty at one time, renders the government of this prison easy, and permits an extremely mild discipline. According to

"Bye-Rules adopted by the Inspectors, September, 1844," it is " provided that the convicts may, at the discretion of the Warden, be allowed to use such books as may belong to the prison and have been approved by the Inspectors." " Writing materials may be allowed on Sundays ; and, when public worship is held in the prison, convicts shall be required to attend, unless prevented by ill health, or by other reasons satisfactory to the Warden."

At the hour I last entered this prison, I found all the convicts, save one, diligently employed at their tables in reading, spelling, writing, and arithmetic. I never saw a better ordered school, or a more studious class of pupils. No person, not informed, could have imagined these to be state convicts, or the apartment to be the working-room of a State penitentiary. I may remark here that, in the event of insubordination and vicious obstinacy, corporal punishment is sanctioned by the inspectors, and privation of food and water is the penalty for wilful transgressors. But though severe measures are sanctioned they are seldom resorted to. The most difficult subjects to hold in control are recommitted convicts from other state prisons. I heard a religious service here, appropriate for the class for whose benefit it was held, by a clergyman who voluntarily gives a part of Sunday to this office in the prison.

The Western State prison of New York, at Auburn, has had a chaplain, appointed and supported by law, since 1835. His duties are arduous in the extreme. I have known no chaplain connected with this prison, whose health has not suffered from efforts to instruct the convicts. The cells (790) are nearly all filled, except occasional vacancies by removals to the hospital, in which the numbers are varying by new cases, and cases discharged.

There is a Sunday school, in which young men from the Theological seminary, and several other citizens, are associated as teachers. But about 260 can be accommodated at one time in the chapel; hence exchanges are allowed from time to time (except in the spelling and reading classes,) which divide the advantages of the school between rather less than 600 of the convicts. Nearly all the prisoners attend regular religious services once on the Sabbath; and short but very impressive services, in the dining hall at the hours of meals, are observed twice daily. The chaplain has free access to the hospital and the shops; but it will be conceived that, where so many need instruction and counsel, it is utterly impossible for one man, devoting all his time and energies to the duty, to meet the moral and mental wants of the prisoners. The Warden especially, and several of the officers, endeavour to unite their aid and influence; but the labors of all, who are employed here, seem to me always to task the time and thoughts to the uttermost. Beside brief interviews during the day, the chaplain, when able, spends from two to four hours on the galleries six evenings of the week, conversing and teaching after lock-up hours. The supply of books at this, as at other prisons, is quite inadequate to the wants of the prisoners. I think there were less than 350 volumes in a condition for use. The Tract and Bible societies have made gifts of tracts and bibles, the latter to be distributed as the convicts leave prison. The State supplies a bible for each cell, and some prayer books.

Of 778 convicts in prison, January, 1845, the chaplain reported ' 156 who could not read when committed; 353 intemperate; 331 lost one or both parents at an early age; 252 left their parents before they were 15 years of age; 301 had been gamblers; 589 were there on their first conviction; 136 on the second; 35 on the third; 14 on the fourth; 1 on the fifth; 83 are under 20 years of age, and 382 between 20 and 30 years.'

There has for several years been increased attention to the instruction of prisoners in the Auburn prison; but it must always be deficient, if imprisonment is to be regarded as reformatory and restoring, as well as punitive, till a new plan for dividing the labor-hours is adopted, and provision made for other teachers to labor in conjunction with the chaplain.

New-York eastern penitentiary, at Sing Sing, has a chaplain appointed and supported by legal enactment. There cannot be at this prison a sufficient attention to moral teaching and mental culture under the present labor system. It will be perceived that the devotion of the whole time of the chaplain to his difficult duties, would afford but a small amount to each convict, there being 868 in the men's prison, and 73 in the women's, at the date of the last year's report, August, 1844. The chaplain reports of his own labors, that

"There is preaching in the men's prison at 9 o'clock on Sabbath morning, and at 10, in the women's prison ; the school being held in each prison during the interim of preaching. The remainder of the day I spend in attending service in the hospital, and in personal conversation with those in the cells who desire it, which generally occupies all the day. The week is spent in visiting the sick in the hospital and elsewhere, and in conducting the correspondence and intercourse of those who have liberty to write to, or converse with their friends."

Books are distributed in the men's prison, at the discretion of the warden and the chaplain, by direction of the inspectors ; this practice, during the last year, has diminished the violations of prison rules, and most of the convicts, who can read, and who can see to read in their confined cells, are eager to possess a book.

Exertions have been made during the past year by the inspectors to promote moral influences, and elevate the moral condition of the prisoners. Books have been contributed through the efforts of intelligent persons interested in the best reform of the prisons ; and these, with the efforts of the officers, have aided the improvement of the convicts. Benefits are especially observed in the women's prison, where the smaller number of prisoners, the less labor required of the convicts, and the exertions of the matrons and assistants, have combined to procure a greatly amended condition.

More than half the prisoners, committed to the Sing Sing prison, are sent from the cities of Brooklyn and New York, where they have become familiar with every degree of vice and crime. The Prison Association in New York propose to direct special care and efforts to advance moral and mental instruction at Sing Sing. The prospects of the prison in this respect are at the present time more hopeful than at any former period.

Of 861 convicts in November last in the men's prison, 536 could read and write; 210 could read; 115 could neither read nor write. Of 73 convicts in the women's prison, 22 could read and write; 30 could read only; 21 could neither read nor write.

A rather *remarkakle* table appears in the last annual report of this prison, where 'the causes for the offences for which they are this year committed to prison,' are thus recorded: "Want of protection in early lfe, 16; intemperance, 192; ditto of wife or of parents, &c. 15; destitution, 112; *no conscience,* 1; *innate depravity,* 26; *insanity,* 7; *imbecility of mind,* 7; *weak principles,* 17; sudden temptation, 40; anger, 11; refuse to answer, 7; innocent, *as they assert,* 149; don't know the cause, 2; for gain, 3; self-defence, 2; jealousy, 1; and evil associations, 253."

It will be seen how serious is the claim of persons under such singular conditions as above-stated, upon the labors of all connected with them, for enlightening and instructing their minds. And not a few appear to be subjects for hospital treatment, rather than prison discipline. But this is a fact not peculiar to the Sing Sing prison. The Warden is zealous to advance, by all possible means, the views of the friends of reform in the men's prison; and the Matron in the women's department has labored earnestly for the last year in this most difficult sphere of duty.

The State prison at Trenton, New-Jersey, like that at Columbus, has no chaplain appointed by law. Voluntary preachers often hold a service on Sunday, but there is less attention to the suitable instruction of the prisoners in this prison than can in any way be excused or accounted for. Heretofore the inspectors have given apparently little thought or influence to the subject, confining their attention to the general direction of the prison, and to financial concerns.

Many of the convicts can neither read nor write: they should be taught: very few have any enlightened ideas of their moral obligations, and need a teacher. Some have received books, but there are too few of these belonging to the prison library to afford much advantage. I ought to add that these wants have awakened interest and attention in the minds of some sensible and influential citizens, and it is reasonable to anticipate an early and effective provision for these deficiencies.*

There is no State Prison in Delaware. The prisoners in the County prisons receive no moral and religious instruction, so far as I can learn. Convicts, sentenced to imprisonment, remain in the county jails, but usually the punishments are summary, at the whipping-post or in the pillory.

The Maryland State Penitentiary, at Baltimore, has no chaplain officially appointed ; but the president of the board of directors states, that

" The prison is open to the clergy of all religious denominations ; and in addition to the regular preaching every Sabbath, in both the men and women's prison, the prisoners are instructed in their moral duties, by ministers of the gospel who visit the prison every week. Those prisoners who do not desire private conversation with religious teachers are exempted ; but all are required to attend service in the chapel. All who can read and desire books are provided with Bibles, Testaments, and moral and religious tracts. The Maryland Tract Society have liberally proposed to establish a library of appropriate books for the use of the convicts, and much good is expected to result therefrom."

The ministers of the Methodist Episcopal Conference are much devoted to the religious instruction of the prisoners on Sundays. The Inspectors report so favorably of the financial concerns of the prison, that one would naturally suppose, as they express a sense of the benefits derived from the diligent labours of voluntary teachers, that they would propose and urge the official appointment of a chaplain, and suggest some modes of procuring for the prisoners the advantages of mental instruction with additional moral culture.

The Penitentiary at Washington, in the District of Columbia, has a chaplain officially appointed, who is interested in his

* Since the first edition of this work, a suitable, and sufficiently large library for present use, has been purchased through the liberality of D. S. Gregory, Esq., of Jersey City, and several gentlemen of Newark. Arrangements are also making for establishing a teacher, uniting the offices of moral instructor and school-master.

duties ; but the arrangements of the prison do not permit sufficient time for the instruction of those convicts who cannot read and write ; though this department is not wholly overlooked. There are services on Sunday, and a Sunday school ; but I cannot commend the custom of making a portion of the convicts teachers for the others. The discipline of the prison may be called close, compared with some others on the same system.

The State prison at Richmond, Virginia, is destitute of a chaplain, and of those general provisions for instruction, which are so important in prisons. Occasionally one service is holden on Sunday by some voluntary preacher. A Bible and slate are furnished in each cell, and small books are occasionally distributed. But few of the convicts have ever had opportunities of moral and mental culture.

The Ohio State Penitentiary, at Columbus, is so totally deficient of the means of moral and mental culture directly imparted, that little remains to be said, after stating the fact. Voluntary preachers, one especially, have toiled here ; yet nothing is done to aid instruction by legislative enactment, and those who make disinterested and self-sacrificing labours in this field find their exertions productive of little benefit, compared with the good results which might be looked for, if a suitable system were adopted for advancing the moral and mental culture of the convicts.

The Western Penitentiary of Pennsylvania, in Alleghany city, has a chaplain, appointed by law, who has daily access to the apartments of the prisoners, where he not only renders religious instruction at proper times, the ' line upon line, and precept upon precept ;' but devotes himself to teaching the untaught in reading and writing. He distributes books, as often as necessary, from the prison library, which is receiving additions from time to time. Religious services are held on Sundays, and I think great care is taken on the part not only of the chaplain, but on that of the warden, to advance the best good of the prisoners. I always found those, who could read, referring to their books with interest. Some gave themselves, during their leisure hours, to a regular course of study in arithmetic, geography, history, &c. Each cell was furnished with a Bible, and most had, in addition, prayer books and hymn books. One of the great advantages of the separate system, is the greater facilities of teachers for imparting instruction, both as to time and place, and the much larger amount of time allowed the prisoner for his own use. The diligent, who accomplish their task early, or timely, have many hours for self-improvement, and this is a stimulant to industry, whose fruits are generally apparent. Of 60 prisoners admitted into the prison in 1844, 41 were intemperate, and 11 moderate drinkers. Most of these, when withdrawn from the temptation of excess in the use of ardent spirits, discover a disposition to improve their minds, and address themselves to their duties with cheerfulness under the direction of their officers.

The Eastern Penitentiary, at Philadelphia, has a chaplain, appointed by law, who commenced his duties in September, 1838. Previous to that period, pious clergymen, and other religious persons visited the prisoners occasionally, and several gentlemen, especially Rev. Messrs. Demmé, Crawford, Irvine, and Wilson, devoted a part of the Sabbath to a religious service. I consider the moral, religious and mental instruction in this prison, which is officially provided, and voluntarily and regularly imparted, more thorough, efficient and complete than is supplied to the convicts of any prison in the United States. And this has been sustained in various ways, since the first occupation of the prison in 1829. The inepctors, in their first report, with timely vigilance urged the appointment with compensation, of a chaplain for the prison. In their second report, 1830, the faithful voluntary services of Rev. Dr. Demmé, and of the Rev. Messrs. Crawford and Wilson, are acknowledged. Besides the usual preaching on Sundays, individuals composing the committee of the Prison Society, visited the prisoners with a view to their spiritual instruction, and useful books were loaned by different persons. In 1830, Dr. Demmé, addressing a letter to the inspectors, says,—

" I rejoice that you regard religious instruction as an integral part of your system. The voice of the unseen preacher produces the most striking and happy effect."

Rev. Mr. Crawford, in 1831, writes,—

" From sermons, exhortations and religious conversations, from time to time held with the prisoners, I am convinced a considerable good has resulted. The moral sense has in some instances been awakened, and religious impressions made."

In 1832, while the inspectors acknowledge the benefits derived from the various voluntary teachers, and especially the good received from ' the Society for alleviating the miseries of prisons,' from ' the Bible Society in supplying bibles, and other religious works,' and from the services of the Rev. Mr. Wilson, who for a long time preached every Sunday, ' much good resulting therefrom,' still press the legislature to appoint a moral instructor, whose duty it shall be to devote all his time to the convicts. The subject was renewed in 1833, and the able services of Mr. Crawford and Mr. Irvine, gratefully attested.

The inspectors, faithful to their trust, in the report of 1833, again appeal to the legislature for additional provision for moral teaching, and repeat their expression of thanks to Messrs. Crawford and Irvine. 1834 finds the same zealous teachers at their good work, In 1835 the legislature are still reminded that they have failed to provide for the services of a chaplain.

In 1836, the Arch-street prison for women being broken up, and the inmates removed to the new County prison at Moyamensing, ' the Association of Women Friends,' divided, and, by invitation, a portion assumed the moral teaching of the women convicts in the County prison, while others, eleven in number, undertook that of the State women-convicts. From that time to the present, these pious and devoted women have labored for the spiritual good and mental culture, of those of their own sex who have, through folly or ignorance, or evil dispositions, become inmates in the Penitentiary. They make stated visits every Monday afternoon throughout the year; and you may see them there seriously and perseveringly engaged in their merciful vocation. Their care extends to the convicts after the expiration of sentences. These ladies read the scriptures, furnish suitable books for the prisoners, give instruction in reading, writing, and arithmetic ; and, what is of great value, because reaching them through a direct influence, instruct them by conversation, suited to their capacity. This association reports in 1836 that ' The prisoners being in separate apartments, are seen apart by their visitors, thus affording opportunity for counsel and instruction adapted to their various circumstances.' The matron is indefatigable in the discharge of her duties, and much interested in the improvement of the prisoners.

In 1836, the inspectors reiterated their demand upon the State for the appointment of a moral instructor, laying more stress upon the good to be imparted by individual teaching, than upon the delivery of weekly discourses, unsustained by constant daily care. The same year, the visiting committee from the legislature report in favor of the wishes of the inspectors, and refer gratefully to the gratuitous labors of the visiting clergy on the Sabbaths.

In the reports for 1837, the claims, urged in preceding years, are repeated ; and, in 1838, after so much importunity, we find appointed the excellent and faithful teacher who has devoted himself so closely to the spiritual interests of the convicts. But let this fact not be overlooked, that, through the stated visits of religious members, both of the men and the women's Prison Society, the preaching of ministers on Sundays (several being always present,) and the visits on other days, of such ministers as were called at the request of the convicts, this prison was by no means in the destitute condition represented by some well-meaning, rather than carefully inquiring writers on the subject.

The direct means of moral and religious instruction now possessed by the prisoners in the Eastern Penitentiary, are these : on Sundays, public service is held, and instruction given often in all, and always in a part of the seven Blocks. Books are distributed to all who can read, beside bibles, hymn-books, and prayer-books, which belong in the cells. On the same day, in addition to collective teaching, the chaplain and the schoolmaster converse with many of the prisoners individually. I have met in the prison, at the same time, ministers of various denominations, gathered each to impart Christian truths, and encourage efforts after improvement. Once a week, on Saturday, the committee from the Prison Society see those who are most in need of their counsels, also the committee from the ' Women's Prison Society,' on Monday. A committee is sent from the German Society to teach those German convicts who cannot speak English. Rev. Mr. Rafferty attends the Catholic convicts, and Mr. Michelbach, the Jews. Instruction in reading, writing, arithmetic, &c. is given by the schoolmaster to those most requiring these lessons. A well-chosen library, established by the benevolence of one of the inspectors, J. Bacon, Esq., and which is gradually increasing through the good offices of those who appreciate this mode of instructing the prisoners, is in continual circulation. A very liberal spirit has always been shown by the regular official visitors in furnishing to the educated convicts, books to advance them in knowledge, and establish regular habits of application and industry. The prisoner's time is his own for improvement, when he has finished his allotted task, which is by no means severe. The chaplain daily, as well as the schoolmaster, goes from cell to cell, adding counsel and exhortation to encouragement and persuasion, and often writing to the friends of any prisoner, who may not be able to do this himself.

It will be seen in the preceding pages, that except in the Eastern Penitentiary, general and moral teaching in the State prisons is insufficiently provided for. In the county prisons, with but few exceptions, it is quite neglected. It is known by all who are acquainted with the actual condition of our prisons, that, where chaplains are appointed and sustained by law, their duties far exceed the measure of their time. On this subject public sentiment is rising, and the prisoner, regarded as an object of commiseration, rather than of anger, is approached by the Christian teacher with kind and earnest efforts to inspire him with truer views of moral obligation, and a reverence for religious knowledge.* It is granted that no endeavor

* Judge Parsons, in his recent charge to the Grand Jury, referring to the want of moral instruction in the Moyamensing prison, says, it is not for us to adduce a train of arguments, in relation to it as one of public policy, or to show that by the continual reformation of criminals, much might be saved by the county, for the support of those committed to prison. In my opinion, a more elevated view becomes us, and higher considerations should be the moving motive which directs

on the part of the teacher, however assiduous, will secure radical reform in the majority of convicts. Against these results we have the almost insurmountable antagonisms of debased habits, low views, lives formed on bad and corrupting influences, a vicious parentage, and an evil neighbourhood, naturally weak understandings with many, and ignorance with a yet larger number. Add, to these adverse circumstances, the debasing influences of our detaining prisons, so destitute of instruction, and permitting indiscriminate companionship. These, combining, have finally brought the convict, not by rapid steps, but through a long career of misdoing, to the State prison. Social rights, just laws, the rule of conscience, and accountability, have not been so much obliterated, as never well understood by the mass of convicted prisoners. Inquire of this large class, which crowd our penitentiaries to their utmost capacity, what have been their moral training, and educational advantages, and how small a number will be found, who have sinned under the full light of wise instruction, early commenced and persevered in!

Enlightened transgressors, and men of considerable intellectual capacity, rarely are found in prisons. These are too adroit, too cunning, to permit themselves to be ensnared by the emissaries of the law. Feeble minds, too infirm of purpose to keep in the straight path, too incapable of reasoning out their truest good and best interest, and many, of constitutionally depraved propensities, chiefly fill the cells of our penitentiaries. The safety of the community requires the restraint of these, and if possible it asks their reformation: to this end, it must supply the means, not by severe and arbitrary punishment, but by firm, consistent discipline, united with carefully-directed modes of instruction. Few have been attracted from an evil to a good life by the severity of their fellow men ; many have been brought to a sense of that knowledge which causeth not to err, by the gracious influences of earnest piety, shining out in the life and

our deliberations. *It is the demand of duty to others. It is the noble principle of charity to the misguided and the unfortunate of our race. It is an appeal to us as a Christian community,* where we would hope the hearts of the people are filled with benevolence, and love to those around them ; filled with the animated inquiry, *how can the most good be done to the distressed ? no matter what is the crime which has produced their misfortune.*

conversation. We too often judge convicts by false standards. We promise, through all reformed prison systems, too much, even under the most favorable modes of administering them. It is not easy to correct a trivial, inconvenient habit for a short time indulged; shall a whole life of wrong and mistake be amended by a few years of imprisonment? Nourish and train rightly the young plants; then, as they grow to maturity, they will not exhibit deformity, and yield unwholesome fruits. While we are unsparingly severe against sin, we must associate mercy and charity with our judgment of the sinner.

The present has been called the age of daring enterprise and bold experiment; this is true, not less in the moral and intellectual, than in the mechanical movements of the world. The long-forgotten theories of past ages, with buried inventions, are revived, modified, applied, and sometimes perfected. It is not wonderful, that, amidst this stirring life, this amazing rush of events, and this business-tossed phase of society, much that is chimerical and unsound, should challenge attention, and engage votaries. Agitated waters throw upon their surface sparkling bubbles, and turbid froth; but the former, in breaking, quickly disappear; and the latter, passing away, bears off impurities, leaving the deep waters wholesome and purified.

The restlessness and excitability of our people must find some escape valve; it is therefore well that the thousand projects and theories of the day should have their experimental life; for experience is a sound and wholesome teacher; and the votaries of plans and systems, which have been tested, whether religious, social, or civil, come quietly to relinquish what they have been allowed to prove useless, when, if opposed, they would cling to error, with all the tenacity of self-will, and the obstinacy of weak-mindedness.

Truth, we know, rests on a basis too solid to be swept away by the rush of error. As the history of the past exhibits the prevalence of truth over that which is false; of right over wrong; of sound reasoning over specious sophisms,—we learn, from these often interrupted, yet finally sure results, a higher faith in human nature, and juster estimates of mutual obligation. Guided by this faith, and more profound sense of duty, we shall gradually place *moral education* in the scale of instruction, from

9

which it has so often been cast out; and so, *moral power* will be increased, this true Archimedean lever, which only can exalt national prosperity to a permanent standard, and secure the duration of free governments.

The restraints of human laws would be less often derided and defied; the laws of God would be less recklessly trampled upon, if public teachers, in studying their several professions, more diligently studied human nature, and more carefully inculcated, in the place of creeds and unessential dogmas of human invention, the holy precepts, illustrated in the life of Jesus Christ. How surely then, if not speedily, would decrease those wrongs and follies, and miseries; those errors and vices, and crimes, which deform society, and break its peace. In the language of one of the wisest instructors of our times, ' *It is the education of the conscience which is chiefly neglected,*' and who may not see that, through this fearful neglect, spring the weeds and the tares, which waste the wheat-fields of the world?

REFORMATION OF PRISONERS.—The reformation of prisoners is a subject often referred to, but generally in such terms as to afford but little satisfactory evidence to the mind of the inquirer. I understand by reformation, not a course of correct conduct in prisons, for often the most accomplished and incorrigible offenders are the least troublesome to their officers while working out their terms of sentence, and converse most satisfactorily with those who have opportunity of verbal communication. Reformation is not embraced in *expressions* of regret for past misdeeds, nor in *professions* of amendment for time to come. I feel justified in reporting only those convicts reformed, who, after discharge from prison, betake themselves to industrious habits, and an honest calling; who, in place of vices, practise virtues; who, instead of being addicted to crime, are observed to govern their passions, and abstain from all injury to others. And I call those converted who unite, with rectitude of conduct in the social and civil relations, a devout and religious spirit, nourished by Christian truth. The evidences of such a reformation of character and life, can only be obtained by years of knowledge and observation of the convicts. The first temptations to go astray after enlargement are, I think, often for a time resisted;

and indeed good resolves are cherished often for considerable periods; but with the majority who are discharged from all our prisons, I know that the opinions on which the fact of reformation is predicated, are exceedingly ill supported by direct evidence. We may hope and wish for the best results, but we do not possess the assurance of them. I know of no person, who has uniformly kept in view so large a number as fifty or one hundred convicts, after their enlargement from any penitentiary, for two, or three, or five consecutive years. Small numbers are occasionally directly heard from; some more generally; but the majority disperse, change their name, and are not traced by those who might be inclined to record their history. We certainly cannot adduce a precise number *reformed*, according to the true meaning of reformation, out of any prison within my personal knowledge, or the reach of my inquiries. I can obtain no general or certain evidence of large numbers. The warden of a penitentiary which has been proposed as a model for others, on the ground of its moral influences, told me, within a few days, that he ' fully believed that ten out of eleven convicts discharged from his prison were reformed.' Asking the reason of this belief he replied that ' they did not come back.' I could not accept that conclusion, and gained no more satisfactory evidence from other officers, or the chaplain. All most sincerely wish this, but the wish stands, I fear, in place of the fact. We claim too much for our prisons, on whichever system established; but I do conscientiously believe that, allowing diligent care and unanimity in promoting moral progress amongst all the officers of prisons on the ' congregated' or ' silent' system, this work is much more difficult and uncertain, than in a well-governed prison on the ' separate' system. From the almost universal custom of the indiscriminate association of prisoners in the county jails, I consider that as yet neither the excellences of the ' silent system,' on the one hand, nor those of the ' separate system,' on the other, have been fairly tried.

I am aware that, both at Sing Sing, Auburn, and Charlestown, from time to time, this subject has engaged attention, but investigation has not been thoroughly carried out. At Sing Sing, according to the report for 1845, of 848 convicts discharged since the spring of 1840, 43 were recommitted; 94

were pardoned; and, of these last, 4 were recommitted; and the chaplain reports that " 100, when last seen and heard from, were doing well.' Now these men are not regularly kept in view, and a part of them have been out too short a time for us to assert that their reformation is complete. The same is the fact in regard to the prisoners referred to in reports at Auburn and Charlestown.

PENITENTIARY SYSTEMS IN THE UNITED STATES.—The two reformed systems of the United States have severally had earnest advocates, claiming for each the highest advantages. It cannot be imagined that any system is perfect as first proposed. Experience in the application, often reveals defects and deficiencies, which, in the beginning, were either not discerned or were overlooked. This has been the case with both our prison systems, the ' separate' and the ' silent' plans. The good men who aided to establish these, did not suppose that no greater advance was to be made. They were glad to possess *good* in place of what was universally declared *bad;* they have been earnest to advance to *better*, and we must hope and trust, that *best* is yet to be developed. This last will not have *origin* in the penitentiaries of the country; it must be derived from *radical* changes in the *early and later* instruction of all children and young persons; in domestic life more wisely regulated; schools more perfectly taught; county prisons remodelled and placed wholly upon a better foundation. When influences, springing from these changes, are felt, we shall be able to have *the best* mode of discipline introduced into all penitentiaries; and we shall see the population of these decrease, as a wider moral sway is brought to enlighten and control society.

Whatever system shall ultimately be adopted, or whether these two so much discussed systems shall be combined into one more perfect than either, the peace and order of society, the duty of the government to offenders, and the obligation of man to man, require that all prisons should be established on just, and on Christian principles. It is plain that the writers who advocate prison reforms, and peculiar forms, will best secure these ends by confining themselves to the practical application of means, with simple, direct, and explicit statements of them. As they consult, or ought to consult, the interests of humanity alone, violent attacks, and partial views of one system, with exaggerated representations of another, should be avoided as subversive of these objects.

We may reasonably hope much from the influence of the clearer and more consistent views in regard to the government and reformation of offenders, which are gaining ground. But too little heed is given to the *prevention* of crime. It would be greatly more worthy of a rising nation, valuing itself on its rapid growth, political freedom, and the diffusion of common school education, to expend more money, and extend a more vigilant care over the young, who, neglected in manners and morals, throng our cities, and large towns, than to vaunt itself continually upon the exceeding excellence of all its institutions. This reiterated national-glorification ; this self-applause, insinuated into every report and address, and yet worse, because more widely disseminated, into every periodical and journal, brings down the standard of morals, and the few, who courageously state the truth in plain terms, are looked upon with suspicion, and almost considered as aspersers when they candidly indicate omissions, or specify mistakes and abuses. It is enough to concede that, as a *new* people, we have begun many things well, and have in few years certainly accomplished much that is creditable to ourselves and our country ; but it should not be forgotten that *more* remains to be performed than has been accomplished ; and more than enough to engage all the benevolent and energetic spirits of the time to labor unfalteringly and with energy, though differing perhaps in the *modus operandi*, to advance the common cause of humanity in a spirit of harmony and good will.

The eminently *practical* spirit which has always directed the movements of the Prison Societies of Philadelphia, ever rich in good works, has accomplished much.*

The enlarged plan and earnestly-directed efforts of the New-

* Addressing a correspondent at Washington, Mr. Haviland very justly remarks, that "it is to the Philadelphia Prison Society that the world is mainly indebted for the most perfect system of prison discipline the wisdom of man has ever produced, and to the State of Pennsylvania, for fully, and at great expense, testing its merits, mankind owes a debt of gratitude."

York Prison Association, alike practical in its aims, are creating for its members an honorable distinction ; awakening the gratitude of many, and the respect of all.

The influence of the Boston Prison Discipline Society has been chiefly exerted, I believe, through the circulation of its Annual Reports. It proposes, as appears from its printed constitution, less direct influence by its members over prison discipline and convicts, than the two first named societies. Some years since a sum was appropriated from the funds of this society, for paying chaplains to serve in the New York and Connecticut prisons. The money thus applied has been repaid, by order of the Legislature of both States, as shown in their public documents.

In remarking upon the Eastern Penitentiary, I do not propose to vindicate the separate system, nor justify those who sustain it. The one is as little needed as the other. Here the many excellences of the system are revealed, and its few defects alike appear ; and the good and upright men who have honestly towards the public, and justly and humanely towards the convict discharged the duties of Governors, Inspectors, and Visitors in this prison, are so well known in public and private life that they need no justification. It is not conceivable that ministers of the gospel, physicians who are especially jealous of the integrity of their profession, officers holding ward over the prison, and inspectors chosen from those who are trusted by their fellow-citizens, together with the humane and benevolent men and women who compose the prison societies, it is incredible that these should combine to uphold a system found, in its working, adverse to the moral, physical, and mental well-being of the prisoners. Allowing that a few might, through prejudice and reluctance to see a favorite plan defeated, be so warped in judgment as to be self-deceived, it is not possible that so many and so variously-constituted minds as are connected with this prison, should combine to deceive, and depart from truth in representation, and from humanity in action. The insinuation which a *very few* holding other and more favorite views, have permitted themselves to make, that the annual reports present partial and false representations of the prison, are too unworthy to deserve comment. Happily for society, and the cause of prison discipline, a liberal and philanthropic spirit now prevails, and is extending an influence which will produce the most salutary results. The friends of the 'separate system' have certainly exercised a remarkable spirit of forbearance under the injurious aspersions of their opponents for many years, judging very rightly that the truth would vindicate itself. It is to be hoped that henceforth the voice of mutual encouragement and good-will, will dignify and distinguish all who engage in these works of mercy towards the fallen and unfortunate, the evil and the debased of our race.

Many persons appear singularly ignorant of the discipline, as well as of the actual condition and employment of prisoners in the Eastern Penitentiary. A vague feeling of horror pervades some minds, when the subject of *separate*, or, as it is often incorrectly called, solitary imprisonment, is spoken of; and they condemn, as inhuman or unjustly severe, a form of imprisonment, of which in fact they have no correct knowledge. To those who cannot visit this prison, and who have no means of large information, it may be interesting to learn that the convicts are uniformly treated with kindness, and regard to their rights as men, not forfeited with their rights as citizens. They are, it is true, in separate confinement, but it is in rooms of good size,* conveniently furnished with reference to preserving habits of neatness and order, and the means of employment for both the mind and the hands. The tasks, which are not burthensome, are accomplished at intervals during the day, the prisoner being left to choose his time : so his work be accomplished, he has liberty to rest, to read, or write, to listen to the counsels of the chaplain, or the teachings of the schoolmaster, and to cultivate in its season the small plat of ground, which the industrious have much pleasure in keeping in order, and in which an hour daily may be spent.† The cells being lighted

* See dimensions of prison-cells, &c., page 44.

† Perhaps the following letter from a convict in the Eastern Penitentiary to his former employer in the country, may be read with interest. It represents the condition of most of the prisoners, and is a literal copy :—

"EASTERN PENITENTIARY, JULY 6, 1844.

DEAR SIR,—I take this oppor'ty of writing to you these few lines, to inform you that I am well ; I was convicted on the 23d of Nov. and was sentenced two years to the Penitentiary, and was brought here on the 27th of the same month, and was confined in a cell, where my employment was picking wool ; it was very lonely work at first I assure you, tho' I was well treated by my keeper. I was just about one month in, when I was moved to another block, under a very fine keeper which treats me with humanity and kindness ; and at evening, afford an opportunity for using the books furnished from the library, and those which belong to the cell ; or accomplishing some little work which the skill or fancy of the inmate may devise.

The prisoner is not therefore solitary, nor quite alone for any long time ; he is separate but it is from fellow convicts, and shut in from the curious gaze of thoughtless visitors. He is not solitary ; for he sees *daily,* three times, the officer who furnishes his meals ; he sees the officer who supplies the working materials, teaches him to work, and receives the work when done ; and he has the means of communicating at any moment with the officer of the corridor ; he sees the warden, the chaplain, the schoolmaster, and the physician and apothecary if not well, any day or hour that he wishes, and some of these by regular diurnal visits. He may see the minister or priest of his choice when he desires ; the committee from the Prison Society, weekly ; the inspectors twice a week. Of course every prisoner is not seen at each visit ; but those who request it are ; and others for whom there is time. The sheriffs see all prisoners from their respective counties when they convey new convicts; and if asked, they, with the permission of the warden, take letters at reasonable intervals, after the first six months. Official visitors are the judges of the courts, the governor and cabinet, members of both branches of the legislature, the members of the acting committee of the

put to sticking a piece of leather,—and then in a few days to making pegs and then to fitting uppers for the shoes, and then my keeper gave me two lasts, and showed me all about making a whole shoe, and by paying great attention how he did it, I went on with the other one, as far as he had finished his, and so on till the shoes were finished, and can now make a middling good shoe, I made 32 pair of large shoes last month, and lay idle part of two days, the cell where I am confined is 16 feet long and about 11 broad, and 12 high. I get plenty to eat, three meals a day, such as bread and meat and potatoes, and mush and coffee and molasses—and soup.—As for the dirty bunch of straw they told me before I came here I should have for a bed, I have a good bed, it is a box-bedstead, two feet high, and a bed tick filled with clean straw and a clean sheet every Sat. and blankets enough to keep me warm the cold winter nights, my keeper told me we had a dreadful cold winter, but my cell was warm and comfortable heated with pipes, my yard is about as large as my cell and I get out about one hour a day. I have right fine corn and beans and cucumbers and various sorts of flowers growing in it. There is two doors where I get into my yard, the outside one is small and of thick plank—the inside one is made of iron bars about two inches apart and through the day the outside one is left open—and I can see in my yard and the air draws through right fine. I have got a hidrant in my cell where I get plenty of water to drink and clean up with. I heard before I was sent here that the cells was very dark, but it is not such a thing,—there is a large window in the top, lighter than the room I was shut up in in Lancaster prison.—I have got a Bible and various sorts of books, and tracts and an almanac and a hymn book which I got from different men that go about visiting the prisons and the minister—and I believe that I have stated to you what is my condition here and by reading which you can see that a prisoner is not so ill treated as folks tell for though liberty exceeds silver and gold and now I wish you to send an answer as soon as possible—I send you all my best respects. Direct to the care of George Thompson, Esq., who is the Warden of the Penitentiary. I see the sheriff of our county and said how I was to all concerned—I want to know if James and Thomas are doing well now.''

Prison Society, the grand jury by courtesy, and occasional visitors by special permission, who have definite objects in acquiring a knowledge of the construction of the prison and its discipline.

The Inspectors report this year, that—

" From sixteen years' experience, and the adoption of such improvements as such experience has suggested, in the practical operation of the Pennsylvania system of prison discipline, separate confinement with labor—all that its founders and early advocates predicted would ensue from its adoption, has been fully and entirely realized. They reiterate the opinion expressed in a former report, that it is ' the only mode by which punishment, discipline, and reform, have been engrafted on a penal code, secured to society and administered to the convict.'

" All the friends of practical philanthropy, in examining this system, rejoice in the great change which is thus being effected in the treatment of the out-cast prisoner—kindness and compassion and a desire for their improvement and reform, accompanied by the means to produce both, are supplanting cruelty and contempt."

The moral instructor at the Eastern Penitentiary, in 1844, testifies as follows :—

" I think the ' separate' system favorable to the development of the intellect. After a short time, a new habit of using the mind is acquired ; the convict begins to reason and reflect. The perceptive faculties are quickened ; the reflective powers are called into action ; the moral nature is awakened ; they listen to my counsel with respect, and are eager to be instructed, whenever I can give them my time. I have observed that separate confinement quickens the memory, and that acquisition, after the first few weeks of application, becomes remarkably easy. I have formed these opinions upon more than six years' experience in the daily office of moral teacher in this prison, and I may add, that the conclusion of the other officers correspond with my own."

The severity of separate confinement to convicts, I have observed, falls chiefly on the most wicked and incorrigible offenders. These, long inured to vagrancy and idleness, living abroad at hazard in conditions of exposure and vicious association, or in poor-houses and jails, choosing the most corrupting companionship, dread solitude as the one great evil. So long as they have associates in prison, they care little for imprisonment. Community of circumstances reconciles them to their condition, or, if not reconciled, they yield to inevitable restraints with stolid indifference, and make themselves callous to reforming influences. On the contrary, those convicts who have been betrayed into crime by sudden outbreaks of passion, by alluring temptations unexpectedly assailing them, or by the mind-beclouding influences of intemperance; those find alleviation of their feelings of remorse and sense of degradation, in the separate cell, where, divided from the hardened and willingly-abandoned offender, they may be sheltered from observation, and, while fulfilling the duties imposed by the rules of the prison, they may also, without disturbance, apply to the serious work of reformation and improvement. It is chiefly convicts of this class who are benefited by the discipline of imprisonment, and who at the period of release, go forth really strengthened to resist the allurements and temptations, which have already proved so fatal to their reputation and their peace.

Mr. Combe, in his Notes on America, remarks of the Eastern Penitentiary, ' that the system of entire solitude, even when combined with labour, and the use of books, with an occasional visit from a religious instructor, leaves the moral faculties in a passive state,' &c. I cannot assent to this proposition; the prisoner does not, it is true, encounter in his cell all the temptations which assail him in the world at large, but his moral faculties are not inactive; and, I think, so far as I have observed, that they are decidedly strengthened. Good temper and good dispositions towards the officers are exercised, and good resolves made and acted upon in most, if not in all, cases.* The prisoner may depart from all these when at liberty, but so do a vast number who have not been the inmates of

---

* The following are two of several letters from prisoners confined under the separate system, in the Western Penitentiary, and were sent after I had spent six days in examining the prison and conversing with the convicts:—

" I have been confined in prison nearly two years; my sentence is for ten years, for coining Spanish quarter dollars. Before I came, and at the time I came I was sick and debilitated; but my health has improved. I have not once been out of my cell;† it is well warmed and ventilated. As to the effect on the mind, I can truly say that solitude has necessarily led me to reflection, particularly on the dissipated habits of my previous life. Reflection, and the aid of books on the subject of total abstinence from intoxicating liquors, has convinced me that I have been a drunkard for the 25 years previous to my coming here. After I had been here some time I lost the desire for stimulents, or, as you called it, I came to ' my right mind,' and I now see that most of my life has been a scene of excitement and confusion through the constant and daily use of fermented and distilled liquors, until in this prison I awoke from my dream. My labor is making heddles for the weavers. It is not so laborious but that I have time for study. Besides the Holy Scriptures and Book of Common Prayer, which I resort to morning and evening daily, I have several works on moral and scientific subjects, which are exchanged monthly for others; a sum in arithmetic or a problem in Euclid, will afford me

† The cells in the Western Penitentiary are constructed without the exercise yards, which are attached to the last-built blocks in the Eastern Prison.

prisons. Mr. Combe also remarks, that " convicts here, after long confinement in solitude, shudder to encounter the turmoil of the world, they become excited as the day of liberation approaches, and feel bewildered when set at liberty. In short, this system is not founded on, nor in harmony with, a knowledge of the physiology of the brain, although it appeared to be well administered." It is true that the day of liberation is to the prisoner one of excitement; but Mr. Combe would not confine this assertion to the prison and system referred to, if he had seen much of prisoners at the times they are discharged from all prisons. I have noticed but small differences, allowing for differences of temperament, in some hundreds of prisoners released from penitentiaries and houses of correction, and my opportunities of observation have been large.

It has been said that Mr. Roscoe was an opponent of this system. I have read letters of Mr. Roscoe, to correspondents in America, and have discovered in them only the sentiments of a humane and excellent mind, not acquainted at all with the practical administration of the system which he condemned,

amusement for hours. I feel satisfied that the solitary system is best adapted to awaken the mind to reflection, and effect a cure of that moral disease called crime.

Very respectfully, madam, W. B."

Observing in one of the cells the following rules for self-government, and learning from the prisoner that he had written and placed them there, I asked him to furnish me a copy, which he did; this, as well as the letter, are literally as follows :—

" RULES wrote by an inmate of the Western Penitentiary, Alleghany, for his own private use :—

Rule 1. I will not willfully violate any known rule of this Institution, but will treat all its Officers, and Chaplain with due respect.

2. I will pay strict attention to the imployment in which I am, or may be engaged.

3. I will devote my leisure hours to study, for the purpose of cultivating a correct moral principle, and improving my mind.

4. I will not harbour the spirit of revenge against my persecutors, " for he who revenges a wrong, put himself on a par with his enemy, but he who magnanimously overlooks an injury, is far above him."

5. I will endeavour to ever keep the final account in view. C. R.........

I find that a strict observance of the above rules has greatly contributed to my happiness; and indeed the happiness of an inmate of this Institution depends almost entirely on his conduct, and disposition: It is for him to say whether he will be happy, or miserable.

When I first entered the Institution It was some considerable time before I could regulate or bring my mind to a balance, but at length I considered that though I was indeed much degraded, yet their was no necessity of making myself more so, and if ever I intended to retrace my steps, that moment was the time to begin.

As I was away from temptation, and from the evil influence of bad company. Considering also that " Man is a bundle of habbits." This thought occurd to my mind. Who knows, but that I may so contract, and consolodate good habbits while I am here that they may remain with me through life. At any rate I am resolved to try. Consequently I applied my mind to study, and to the cultivation of those finer feelings which should occupy the breast of every inteligent being, endeavouring as mutch as possible to cast behind me former associations which were vicious in their nature, and to press forward to better things which were before. And at the same time trying as much as possible to cultivate kind, and forgiving feelings towards those whom I thought had injured me. And I find that the above course has greatly contributed to my peace, and happiness. I would also observe, that my progress has been accelerated at every step by the kind, and humane treatment which I have received from the officers of the Institution, whom I shall ever remember with grattitude. C. R........."

and condemned only because he had not witnessed its results. Had this good man lived to visit the Pentonville prison, in his own country, he would have been one of the most earnest advocates of the system. When Mr. Roscoe wrote on this subject, the Eastern Penitentiary was not even built, nor the present system precisely determined.

Mr. Dickens's opinions attracted some notice for a time. His pages are certainly written with effect, but belong to the fancy sketches which have so much interested the readers of his attractive works. A visitor to the Eastern Penitentiary might come often, and remain long, without realizing the supposed facts represented in the following passage : ' The dull repose and quiet that prevails, is awful. Occasionally there is a drowsy sound from some lone weaver's shuttle, or shoemaker's last, but it is stifled by the thick walls, and heavy dungeon doors, and only seems to make the general stillness more profound.' I certainly never witnessed confusion in this prison, during the fifteen consecutive days I spent in studying its discipline, and in examining the cells, nor during many subsequent visits ; but the sounds inevitably produced by the many looms, and other mechanical labors of the inmates, certainly left me little to remember of " dull repose," and " awful quiet." And so of the descriptive sketches which follow.

I am not so earnest an advocate of the " separate system," as to desire its adoption in all states and countries, and under all and any circumstances, where prisons are needed. I do not conceive that prisons so disciplined, would be desirable either in Egypt and Turkey, or in Spain and Spanish America. I have given, when it was asked, within the past year, my opinion against the adoption of this system in the West Indies. But in any and all countries, *where similar* influences, and an equally efficient and beneficent administration can be brought to bear, as in the Eastern Penitentiary, and in the Pentonville prison in England, I should for the sake of humanity, and a just care which society owes to the unfortunate offender, desire to see this system widely studied, understood, and adopted. The separate system admits in all the parts of its administration, a more direct application and exercise of Christian rule and precepts, than any other mode of prison government. It brings the officer into communication with the prisoner, not as the commander, and not as the guard, watchful and wary, noting of necessity each movement and act; but as the kind governor and attendant, seldom called on to exercise other than beneficent influences, performing his duties with cheerfulness and good-will. The inevitable frequency and severity of punishments in other prisons, where the convicts work in gangs, is avoided here. The best faculties, feelings and perceptions of the prisoner are called out and exercised, while the evil are for the most part left dormant. The governor of a prison, on the silent system, though of equally good judgment, and humane sensibilities, and equally disposed to all that is really kind, cannot govern his prison, and maintain as mild discipline, and nourish as good dispositions in his prisoners, as can the governor of a prison on the separate system. Without entering upon arguments and details, I think this must be apparent to all persons conversant with these subjects. So far as I have heard or read, the objections advanced against the separate system are not profound nor real; they are either unessential, or they exist only in the imagination, and are not to be found when the prisoners are inspected. I think this a far too serious question, and too nearly affecting the condition of many human beings, to permit myself to study the subject with haste, or as I believe governed by any motives save those which seek the best good of a class, so numerous in our country. I have sought for the truth earnestly. I think I cannot have been deceived or mistaken in the facts, on which I rest favorable conclusions.*

* Since the first edition of this pamphlet was sent to press, I have read 'the charge of Judge Parsons to the Grand Jury of the Court of Quarter Sessions, for September, 1845. I quote from it the following passage, which relates to the Pennsylvania prison system. "The subject of prison discipline for years, occupied the attention of many of the most distinguished and philanthropic men in Pennsylvania. The great object of these noble efforts was, to adopt a system which it was thought was the best calculated to maintain the dignity of the laws, and in the most humane manner, endeavor to reform the criminal, and, at the same time deter others, by a mild, but efficient punishment, from the commission of offences. *The system of separate confinement, with labor, which has been adopted in this State, for the punishment of criminals, 1 believe is one of the best that has ever been devised by the genius of man. This individual opinion is expressed after a very close observation of its effects for the last five years, during*

It is often objected to the separate system, that communication between the prisoners is not entirely prevented.— I do not think that communication from cell to cell is always cut off; but it can never (except by infidelity of the officers of the corridors) be carried on in any way likely to produce much evil; and all know that in prisons on the Auburn plan, the most complete mutual knowledge is possessed, and that to a great extent. Communication in fact, in most of these prisons, as at Charlestown, is almost as free as at a county jail. The prisoners are perfectly familiar with each other's history. and with many circumstances not occurring in the shops and yards. Nor do I think that any closeness of discipline can prevent all communication, at least in the largest prisons. I know well this has never been effected, either at Auburn or Sing Sing. At Wethersfield, where the discipline is close, and the prisoners fewer, it may be done more successfully.

Under the silent system, writes M. Fregier:—

" The prisoners succeed, by force of cunning and address, in communicating with each other by whispers and by signs. They are so skilful in deceiving the watchfulness of their keepers, that the more perverse have been known to devise, with their comrades, plans of mischief, to be executed on their discharge. The incessant struggle between the convicts and those who exercise the repressive power, is such that it tends constantly to irritate those upon whom that power is continually operating, and to provoke them to all the mischiefs and dangers of revolt. This consideration, and the fact that the keepers must weary and flag in their watchfulness, has begot a general belief that this system, however for a time enforced, generally ends in a certain degree of tolerance in the use of speech. M. Demetz, who accompanied M. Blouet, the architect, to the United States, to study the progress of the science of prisons, since the interesting publication of Beaumont and De Tocqueville, upon the condition and government of the penitentiaries of that country, in a report made by him to the Minister of the Interior, abounding in facts and useful documents, asks,—' Where are we to find men who can be charged with maintaining such a discipline, who will not in the event become either cruel or negligent ?' In Great Britain, the *silent system* has been attempted without resort to the aid of *corporal* punishment. The experiment has signally failed, and recourse has been had to force to conquer the refractory.

which period, I have been most of the time engaged in the administration of our criminal law, and a very close observer of the effect of this system upon those who have been sentenced."

" At Cold Bath Fields, where the infliction of corporal punishment is not permitted without a previous examination and hearing of the case, the director, a man of remarkable capacity and intelligence, has not less than sixty reports to hear every morning; for the prisoners, as well as the keepers, are permitted to bring up their complaints. In 1836, notwithstanding all the efforts for the good government of this establishment, there were 5,138 chastisements inflicted for swearing and talking. In 1838, the number of such inflictions had risen to 9,750, in a number of convicts amounting to 13,812.

" In the house of correction at Wakefield, also on the silent system, the punishments during the same year, numbered 12,445, in a population of 3,438. Finally, in all the other prisons of England, in which the silent system prevails, they have counted 54,825 punishments in a total population of 109,405.

" These results are so much the more remarkable, as they show that the classification of the prisoners, which forms a part of the regulations in the English prisons, has been insufficient, combined with the silent system to prevent verbal communications.

" Mess'rs Crawford and Russell, inspectors-general of the English prisons, in summing up, in their Report, the objections raised to the law of silence, thus answer those who think that a hasty word thrown out by a convict, cannot be fraught with evil. ' Admitting that one word is not as mischievous as ten, does it follow that the single word which is heard, may not be one of a series uttered on different days. and altogether intended to form a communication of dangerous import? Is it necessary to the communication of frequent meanings that many words be used? May not a gesture contain a proposition, a project, a discourse? We have a thousand examples of prisoners under the most rigorous laws of silence, who, at the end of four weeks, knew the names and the minutest particulars of the imprisonment of their companions in the yard or shop."

An Inspector of the French prisons, Moreau Christophe, says of the " separate" system, as adopted in Phildelphia, ' it is the only system that fulfils all the conditions of a complete penal discipline. The Viscount Bretignères says, " Both the moral and material reform of our prisons is a social necessity, and can only be effected by a revision of the criminal law and an entire adoption of the system in force in the Eastern Penitentiary at Philadelphia." Dr. Julius, so well known as earnestly devoted to the reform of prisons in Prussia, having given himself months carefully to visit and examine our prisons, writes as follows :—

" I declare candidly that, upon an examination of my own conscience and the knowledge I have acquired of the different systems of prisons in Europe and America, none has appeared to me to present so much equity and justice in the infliction of punishment, or affords so many chances of reformation, as that of solitary confinement, combined with the regular visits of the officers of the prison, such as the inspectors, governor, chaplain, and medical men. I say *chances* of reformation, because human efforts are necessarily limited."

MM. De Beaumont and De Tocqueville, commissioners from France to the United States in 1831, also report in favor of the Eastern Penitentiary, as offering an example of humane and judicious administration, worthy to be imitated. "The Philadelphia system," say they, "is the very system, the discipline of which offers the least embarrassment. There are some persons who consider the order established in it to be complicated, organized with difficulty, and maintained with trouble. They are, in our opinion, greatly mistaken." M. De Metz and M. Blouet, commissioned by the French Government, in 1836, for a similar purpose, corroborate, and repeat the favorable opinions of their precursors.

MM. Neilson and Mondelet, from Canada West, commissioned by the provincial government to visit and report upon the Penitentiaries in the United States, express their preference for the Pennsylvania system, (in a broad statement of reasons, too much in detail to be introduced here,) above that which exhibits the working-gangs on the silent plan. The Auburn plan has, however, been adopted at Kingston, C. W. At the season of my journeys to examine the prisons in the British provinces, this prison was not completed, though occupied by a large body of convicts.

Mr. Crawford, commissioner from England, authorized to visit the prisons of the United States, thus refers to the Eastern Penitentiary:

"Upon a careful review of every part of the Eastern Penitentiary, after seeing the whole, and examining a considerable number of the individuals confined in it, I have no hesitation in declaring my conviction, *that its discipline is a safe and efficacious mode of prison management; and that it has no unfavorable effect upon the mind or health,* and with the addition of moral and religious instruction, [introduced on the present more complete plan since Mr. Crawford's visit,] solitary imprisonment, thus enforced, may be rendered powerfully instrumental not only in deterring, but also in reclaiming the offender."

In Europe this system has been studied and discussed, and, in some countries adopted, either in whole or in part. With a view of *extending* the general adoption of the separate system in France, the erection of a model prison at Versailles was determined upon for convicted prisoners. That locality was chosen from its vicinity to Paris, thus opening to the government officers an opportunity of becoming acquainted with the working of the system. Since that period several prisons have been established on the principle of separation, chiefly for untried offenders.

M. Delessert reports of the prison in Paris for juvenile delinquents on the separate system, as follows:—' The prison contains 550 cells, 436 being for convict occupancy. This system prevents the reciprocal inoculation of vicious propensities, allows the exercise of individual action on each prisoner, and affords opportunities of exhortation, instruction and labor, without the external obstacles which other systems present.' M. Delessert speaks of the sanitary influences of the separate system upon the health of the convicts : only five or six per cent. being on the sick list, where formerly on the social system, there were ten or eleven per cent. on an average. ' The juvenile criminals are employed as jewellers, buckle-makers, gilders, joiners, turners, brass-chain makers, locksmiths, metallic button makers, and stocking weavers.'

' As to the expense, it is shown that the separate system with all its advantages, here costs but about £1 16 . per annum for each prisoner more than the social system. The superior benefits more than compensate for the difference in the cost.' The question of expense I do not think it worth while to discuss. It having been shown both in England and in Pennsylvania, that it need not much exceed that of the opposite plan. The prison buildings alone, at Auburn, cost New York *six hundred thousand dollars.*

The following extract from the ' *Exposé des Motifs*,' submitted to the Chamber of Peers, by M. Duchatel, Minister of the Interior, for the introduction of the separate system into France, may be read with interest :—

CHAMBER OF PEERS. *Session of June* 10, 1844.

* We now submit to your deliberations the proposed law concerning Prison Discipline already adopted by the Chamber of Deputies.

This question, for half a century, has occupied the most enlightened governments of Europe and America. Numerous experiments have been made in the United States, in Switzerland, England and Germany.

The reform of our prisons is one of the objects which most require the care of government; the expression of public opinion makes it our duty to give to this problem, our most serious attention. Remedies in fact for the vices of the present discipline, must be found in a new discipline which better agrees with the spirit of the laws, the state of morals, and regard for the public security. It is essential to the first interests of society that the principle of intimidation, which is the basis of all penal law, should not be weakened. To give force to this principle, while preserving the prisoner from fatal corruption is the object of the proposed law.   *   *   *   *

The discipline which we propose to establish in all the prisons as a general rule, with a few exceptions which we shall point out hereafter, is that of solitary confinement.

It is well known that all plans for reforming prisons belong to two principal systems; one, called the Auburn system, admits solitude only during the night, with intercourse and labor in silence during the day;

"CHAMBRE DES PAIRS. *Séance du* 10 *Juin*, 1844.

* "Nous venons soumettre a vos délibérations le projet de loi sur le régime des prisons, déjà adopté par la Chambre des Députés.

"Cette question, depuis un demi-siecle, occupe les Gouvernements les plus éclairés de l'Europe et de l'Amérique. De nombreuses expériences ont été accomplies aux Etats-Unis, en Suisse, en Angleterre, et en Allemagne. La réforme de nos prisons est un des objets qui se recommandent le plus à la sollicitude du Gouvernement; les avertissements de l'opinion nous faisaient un devoir de porter sur ce problème social notre attention la plus sérieuse. Il importe, en effet, de remédier aux vices du régime actuel par un régime nouveau, qui réponde mieux à l'esprit de la loi, à l'état des mœurs et aux besoins de la sécurité publique. Il importe aux premiers intérêts de la société que le principe d'intimidation qui est la base de toute pénalité ne soit pas affaibli. Rendre à ce principe sa force, tout en préservant les détenus d'une corruption funeste, telle est la pensée du projet de loi. *   *   ⋆

"Le régime que nous proposons d'établir dans toutes les prisons, comme règle générale, sauf quelques exceptions, que nous indiquerons plus tard, est celui de l'emprisonnement individuel.

"On sait que tous les plans de réforme des prisons se rapportent à deux systèmes principaux : l'un connu sous le nom de système d'Auburn, n'admet l'isolement que pendant la nuit, avec la vie commune et

the other called the Philadelphia system, which has been in operation for fourteen years in the prison in that city, is that of complete separation of the prisoners both night and day. We will explain briefly the motives which have determined our choice, previously observing, that in the proposed law, which we have the honor to present to you, we have made considerable modifications, to adapt it to practice, (according to our manners and national character,) that one of the two systems, to which we have given the preference.

The system which requires solitude only during the night, with labor in common during the day, does not produce a real reformation; it prevents perhaps the most violent disturbances, but there its efficacy ceases. The rule of silence, upon which it rests, it is impossible to enforce, and the very considerable expenses which its adoption would involve, would not be compensated by sufficient advantages.

The official reports in England and the United States show, that in the prisons where this system is in operation, inspection is almost insurmountably difficult; silence is very imperfectly maintained, notwithwithstanding the frequent use of disciplinary punishments, which include the use of the whip, a punishment which is repugnant to our national feelings. The great number and zeal of subordinate officers, the energetic will of the directors cannot in fact prevent improper communication between the prisoners, either in the hours of exercise, at

le travail en silence pendant le jour ; l'autre, appelé système de Philadelphie, en vigueur depuis quartorze ans dans la prison de cette ville, est celui de la séparation complète des détenus entre eux, soit pendant la nuit, soit pendant le jour. Nous exposerons brièvement les motifs qui ont déterminé notre choix, en faisant observer tout d'abord que, dans le projet de loi que nous avons l'honneur de vous présenter, nous avons notablement modifié, pour l'adapter à la pratique, d'après l'état de nos mœurs et le caractère national, celui des deux systèmes auquel s'est arrêtée notre préférence.

" Le système qui n'admet l'isolement que pendant la nuit, avec le travail en commun pendant le jour, n'opère pas une véritable réforme : il prévient peut-être les désordres les plus grossiers ; mais là s'arrête son efficacité. La régle du silence, sur laquelle il repose, est d'une observation impossible, et les dépenses considérables que son application entraînerait ne seraient pas compensées par des avantages suffisants.

" Les rapports officiels, en Angleterre et aux Etats-Unis, font connaître que, dans les prisons où ce système est en vigueur, la surveillance est d'une difficulté a peu prés insurmontable ; le silence y est maintenu très-imparfaitement, malgrè le fréquent emploi des punitions disciplinaires, qui comprennent la peine du fouet, châtiment que repoussent nos mœurs. Le grand nombre et le zèle des employés, la volonté énergique des directeurs, ne peuvent empêcher, en effet, des communi-

table, or in the midst of the labors, which themselves so frequently facilitate the violation of law, and furnish a thousand opportunities of eluding the vigilance of the keepers.   *   *   *

The system of separation, night and day, is the only one, the advantages of which are real and satisfactory. In this system discipline and good order are sustained without difficulty.   *   *   *

Objections of various kinds have been raised against solitary confinement. We will confine ourselves to the two principal. 1st. It is said to involve too great expense. 2d. It is accused of disordering the mental faculties, of impairing the health, and even of causing death. These objections are grave; *but it is easy to answer them.*

It is very true, that it is more expensive to build a prison, constructed for the system of separation in cells by night and day, than one appropriated to living in common; but in reality the increase of expense stops there; for it is not correct to say that the number of attendants must be more considerable, or the labor necessarily less productive. In England, the number of attendants has of necessity been constantly increased, in houses where the Auburn system is in operation; and as to the labor, the example of the Roquette in Paris proves, that it can easily be arranged in prisons on the solitary-confinement system. Besides, it must not be lost sight of, that the proposed law

cations coupables entre les détenus, soit pendant les promenades, soit à table, soit enfin au milieu de ces travaux, qui facilitent si fréquemment eux-mémes l'infraction de la règle, et qui fournissent mille occasions d'échapper à la vigilence des gardiens.   *   *   *

" *Le régime de la séparation des détenus pendant la nuit et pendant le jour est le seul dont les avantages soient réels et suffisants.* Dans ce système la discipline, et le bon ordre sont maintenus sans effort. **

" On a élevé contre le régime de l'emprisonnement individuel des objections de diverse nature. Nous nous arréterons à deux principales : 1° on lui reproche d'entraîner des dépenses trop considerables ; 2° on l'accuse de porter le trouble dans les facultés mentales, de détruire la santé, de causer même la mort. Ces objections sont graves, *mais il est facile d'y répondre.*

" Il est très-vrai qu'une prison construite pour le systéme cellulaire de nuit et de jour, coûte plus cher à bâtir qu'une prison appropriée à la vie commune ; mais là se borne, en réalité l'accroissement de la dépense, car il n'est pas exact de dire que le nombre des employés doive y être plus considérable, ni que le travail y soit nécessairement moins productif. En Angleterre, on a été obligé de multiplier de plus en plus les surveillants dans les maisons où le système d'Auburn est en vigueur, et, quant au travail, l'exemple de la maison de la Roquette, à Paris, prouve qu'il peut-être facilement organisé dans les prisons soumises au régime de la séparation complète des détenus. Au reste, il ne faut pas perdre de vue que le système du projet de loi doit avoir in-

would certainly not tend to diminish the number of crimes, and consequently that of criminals; and as we propose, also, in our calculations of the length of punishments, to take into consideration what is added in severity, it is evident that we thus succeed in a two-fold manner in reducing the number of those prisoners, it is necessary to watch over and control. The diminution of the annual and ordinary expenses, without speaking of the moral advantages, tends to balance the expenses which the establishment at first requires.

As to the objection relative to the health and life of the prisoners, it is refuted by the numerous facts which the experience of twenty years has collected. It is now proved that the fears entertained upon this point were very much exaggerated, and not well founded. Imprisonment is doubtless, in some degree, always injurious to health and longevity, as well as to tranquillity of mind; but this is true of all systems; it is an inevitable result and effect of punishment; it is one of its conditions; and it is sufficient to assure the Legislator, that solitary confinement has, in this connection, no more injurious consequences than any other system. No conclusion can be drawn from a few cases, which form exceptions to a general rule.

The superior advantages of the separate system have been strongly maintained in *Belgium* by M. Ducpetiaux, the Inspector-general of prisons. The Belgian government has ordered the introduction of the " separate system" in the celebrated

failliblement pour résultat de diminuer le nombre des délits et des crimes, et, par suite, celui des détenus : et comme nous nous proposons en outre, de tenir compte, dans le calcul de la durée des peines, de ce qui est ajouté en sévérité, il est évident qu'on arrive ainsi, par un double effet, à réduire la population de détenus, qu'il s'agit de surveiller et d'entretenir. La diminution des dépenses annuelles et ordinaires vient donc, sans parler des avantages moraux, et atténuation des charges qu' entraîne le premier établissement.

" Quant à l'objection relative à la santé et à la vie des détenus, elle est combattue par les faits nombreux qu'une expérience de vingt années a permis de recueillir. Il est aujourd'hui démontré, que les craintes qu'on avait pu concevoir à cet egard, étaient très-exagérées et ne reposaient pas sur des bases solides. L'état d'emprisonnement est sans doute, dans une certaine mesure, toujours nuisible à la santé, à la longévité, comme à la tranquillité d'esprit ; mais cela est vrai dans tous les systèmes : c'est un effet et une suite inévitables de la peine, c'est une de ses conditions ; et il suffit, pour rassurer le législateur, que l'emprisonnement individuel n'ait pas, sus ce rapport, des conséquences plus fâcheuses qu'un autre régime. On ne saurait rien conclure de quelques cas tout à fait exceptionnels." * * *

Maison de Force at Ghent, where the Auburn system originated, and has long been practised. A new wing for 300 prisoners, has been erected for trial of this system. In Prussia, in consequence of the investigations and reports made by Dr. Julius, the king has ordered the construction of four prisons on the separate system, namely, at *Berlin, Konigsburg, Munster* in *Westphalia*, and *Ratibor;* these adopt the model of the excellent prison at Pentonville. In 1835, under the orders of Count Skarbeck, a separate prison was constructed at *Warsaw*, to receive nearly 500 prisoners.

The Diet of 1839 and 1841, in *Hungary*, having resolved to introduce an uniform system, the commissioners decided *in favour of the separate system*, and submitted a plan for *ten penitentiaries* for as many districts, into which they propose that the whole country should be divided. The council sitting at Pesth drew up a penal code, providing that all *corporal* and *capital* punishments should be abolished, and that publicity should be adopted in all criminal proceedings. In *Denmark* the government commission have declared in favor of the *separate* system. In *Sweden* the Crown-prince is one of the most zealous advocates of the *separate* system, and its discipline is to be introduced at *Stockholm, Fahlun, Gefle, Carlistad, Manstad, Linkoping*, and *Christianstad*. In *Norway* the Storthing has voted £40,000 for the erection of a prison on the separate system, capable of receiving 238 criminals in the vicinity of *Christiania*.

The board of directors of prisons in *Scotland*, being desirous of providing for each county, accommodation for its criminal prisons on the *separate system*, have adopted measures for the accomplishment of this object.

The legislative council in France have expressed the opinion, that the principle of separation by day and by night, ought to be extended to all prisons, for prisoners before trial. The department of the Seine has voted three millions of francs for the constructinn of 1200 separate apartments for all the untried prisoners of Paris.

June, of the present year, (1845) writes Dr. Julius from Hamburg, has been decided on for opening the men's prison at Cologne, to receive nearly 200 prisoners. This prison is founded strictly on the separate system. Other prisons on the same plan are advancing to completion.

In Switzerland the *silent* system has been introduced, and variously modified at Lausanne, &c. Geneva has ordered a prison on the *separate* system. In Germany, the Pentonville-prison near London, has been adopted as the general model for the new prisons. At Frankfort on the Maine, the committee appointed to investigate the subject of reform in prisons, unanimously decided in favor of the Pennsylvania system. At Hamburg, the old prison having been destroyed during the great fire, is to be replaced by one on the same plan as that at Frankfort. In the Grand Duchy of Baden, where, some years ago, a prison was built at Bruchsal on the Auburn plan, it has been decided to build another on the separate system. This has been urgently recommended by Dr. Deiz, the gover-nor of the Bruchsal prison, who from his official experience, has had ample opportunity of becoming acquainted with the silent system. Already, in France, more than thirty prisons are in progress of construction, or completed, on the Pennsylvania plan of separate imprisonment. These are chiefly to be occu-pied by prisoners before trial. In 1843, a division of the military prison at Alost in Belgium was built on the separate plan. Professor der Tex and the philanthropic Suzingar, are successfully advocating the separate system. ' The latter, who may be styled the Howard of Holland, has been conscientiously opposed to separate imprisonment, but has now become one of its most intelligent and able defenders.' Three (on the separate system) are already occupied in Poland. In Baden the female penitentiary on the Auburn plan, according to Dr. Julius, did not answer expectations. M. Villemain has been commissioned to proceed from Pays de Vaud to Germany and France, to inspect the new prisons on the separate system.

Jurists and physicians in Italy, the Lombard-Venetian states, and adjacent territories, have instituted diligent inquiries into the condition of the metropolitan and provincial prisons, and commissioners have been named to prosecute inquiries through-out France, England, and the United States, respecting the condition of prisons, and the practical working of the modern reformed systems. The Marquis Torrigiani, having visited and carefully examined the prisons in the United States, zealously advocates the Pennsylvania system in Tuscany. On this subject, light is breaking on the civilized nations of Europe. And, while we acknowledge the age in which we live to be charged with a terrible amount of vice and crime, we see with rejoicing that it is also marked by great virtues and vast objects, reaching to the real good of all mankind. Noble minds, in all enlightened countries, with zeal and discrimination, are devoting talents and influence to check the progress of crime, and restore offenders, through moral culture and religious influence to duty and a better life.

In Sardinia, attention has been directed to the same subject, and some new prisons have been established at Turin and Alexandria, in order to test the silent system upon juvenile offenders in the former city, and adult criminals in the latter.

The inspector general of prisons in Ireland reports, that in the female penitentiary at Dublin, the women are separated during most of the day when at work; and as soon as a sufficient number of well ventilated cells shall be constructed, they will carry out the system more completely. The matron reports the number of recommittals greatly decreased. The accounts from Sligo are similar, and the prison on the South Circular Road, near Dublin, for male prisoners, has partially adopted the separate system. In Belfast, the model of the Pentonville prison has been adopted in a prison designed to receive 300 prisoners, and of course is strictly on the separate system. It is to be the model prison for Ireland. I do not learn what amount of moral instruction is associated with other reformatory measures; but infer, that there, as well as elsewhere, it still is too little regarded as one of the chief means of producing good under the circumstances of personal restraint.

Mr. Hill, in the third report of the inspectors of prisons in Scotland, remarks, that except in case of excess in the number of prisoners above present accommodations for them, there are in Glasgow, Aberdeen, Paisley, Ayr, Dundee, Montrose, and Lerwick, prisons where the *separate* system is fully carried out; and in Edinburgh, Lanark, Hamilton, Greenock, Perth, and Rothesay, separation is partially adopted. At Perth is one prison, since March, 1842, in which the separate system is strictly conducted. The physician remarks in one of the reports, that " the benefits of this system are every day becoming more apparent; and the prisoners themselves say, ' We have no quarrels; our cells are our own; we have no swearing; and are no longer liable to be punished for the faults committed by others.' The fact of their having no companions to converse with; no one to harden the heart by deriding the appearance of contrition, renders the prisoners more submissive, more willing profitably to occupy their minds; and, at the same time, disposes them to look forward with impatience for the visits of their officers, and to hear them on such occasions with greater respect, and, in not a few instances I might safely say, with more affection, than would probably happen under different arrangements." Alterations are proceeding in various prisons in Scotland, in view of promoting moral discipline.

The prison at Pentonville, two and a half miles from London, is conducted on the Pennsylvania system, and is constructed with all the recent improvements in heating, supplying water, and thorough ventilation. This prison is excellently governed. The ignorant are taught to read and write. Prayers are offered daily. Sunday is occupied in preaching, religious instruction, and reading.* The chaplain has the aid of a chief teacher, and three assistants, in conducting the classes which receive daily instruction in the various branches of common school education. Pentonville is a prison ' of instruction and probation,' preparatory to transportation to Van Dieman's Land. The limit of

---

* I have, while writing the above, received, through the ready attention of a friend, the Third Report of the Pentonville prison, and make the following extracts. "The MENTAL condition of the entire body of the prisoners has been highly satisfactory. (Daily average 456.) During the past year, and up to the present time, no case of insanity, hallucination, or mental disease of any kind, has occurred among the prisoners. This is more remarkable and satisfactory, inasmuch as it has been ascertained, subsequently to their admission, that there existed an hereditary predisposition to insanity in the case of twenty-three of the prisoners, received into this prison."

The Medical Officer writes, "There is a general improvement in manner and address, indicative of intellectual advancement, very strikingly shown among the prisoners who have been the longest in confinement; and an increased alacrity, and desire to excel in work, is, in most cases, the early result of this system of confinement."

imprisonment is therefore in this prison eighteen months. The heating and ventilation I understand to be better than that of any prison hitherto constructed.

In Reading, county of Berkshire, a prison is now completed and occupied, having 300 cells constructed for *separate* confinement at labor. At Bristol the old prison has been re-modelled, and fitted to the *separate* labor system. At Bedford a new prison is erected; it contains 500 cells on the Pennsylvania plan, with such improvements as have been added at Pentonville.*

HOUSES OF REFUGE FOR JUVENILE OFFENDERS.

Houses of Refuge are established for Suffolk county, Mass. at South Boston; for New-York city and state, in the city of New-York; and for Philadelphia city, and the state, at Philadelphia.

The House of Reformation for juvenile offenders, at South Boston, was formerly an independent institution; but, about four years since was made a branch of the House of Industry; the management being committed to the same governing officers. The following extract from the report of the directors, for April, 1845, may serve to show the *general discipline, &c.*

"It is nearly four years since the House of Reformation for Juvenile Offenders was made, in some respects, a part of the House of Industry, and its management committed to the same officers. This department occupies the west wing of the House of Reformation building, where the accommodations are ample for 75 or 80 boys. The average number the year past, has only been about 50. A considerable number of these, it is expected, may soon be apprenticed under favorable circumstances.

"The children in the House of Reformation are kept under a constant, but mild discipline. They are well fed and clothed. Four hours in each day they are in school, giving attention to the common and useful branches of education. Such as have the physical strength are required to labor six hours daily. Employment and constant supervision are much relied on as means of effecting a moral reformation in character. Sufficient time is allowed for ablutions, devotional

---

* The information given above, respecting foreign prisons, I have received chiefly through the courteous attention of correspondents in Europe.

exercises, meals, recreations and sleep. Many of the boys have a taste for useful reading, and highly value their privilege of access to a good library.

"In reference to this department, the inspectors of prisons, in their last semi-annual Report, Dec. 1844, remark, 'this House continues to be a scene of order, decorum, neatness, active industry, cheerful obedience, religious observances ; successful instruction in the branches of education, taught in the common schools of the Commonwealth ; some cultivation of the art of vocal music, and due recreation. This Institution has a most salutary influence in withdrawing children from the haunts of vice and crime, and reclaiming them, and putting them in the way of becoming respectable men and useful citizens ; and it is matter of regret that many more of the children who are permitted to spend their time in the streets in idleness, in learning and practising mischief, vices, and petty offences, are not brought within its beneficent discipline, instead of being left to qualify themselves, by degrees, for the House of Correction.'

"It may not be generally known, especially by parents who neglect the salutary control of their children, that the Municipal and Police Courts have not only the power to commit to the House of Reformation, children and youth convicted of serious offences, but also ' any child or children that live an idle and dissolute life,' their parents being dead, ' or, if living, *do from vice, or any other cause, neglect to provide suitable employment for, or exercise salutary control over such child or children.*' A greater regard to this law, without crowding the House of Reformation, might induce parents to a better care of their offspring, and save many from moral degradation."

The causes of commitment are as follows : ' Larceny, stubbornness, idleness, common drunkenness, vagrancy, pilfering, and passing counterfeit money. The boys are chiefly employed on contracts for shoe-making.

The east wing of the commodious building, originally constructed for the House of Reformation solely, is now occupied by the boys of the Boylston school, about one hundred in number, between the ages of six and thirteen. These boys, as well as those of the west wing, appear to me to be cheerful and in health. Their deportment is orderly, and their advantages in most respects good for their condition. The directors report, that

"In this interesting department, under faithful instruction and care, are boys of humble origin, but promising capacity, who are making commendable progress in common school studies. If placed at proper age in suitable families and employment, their future prospects of respectability and usefulness are perhaps as fair as that of any other school, or class of lads."

THE FARM SCHOOL.—The following extracts from the report of the Farm School will show that some measures are wisely adopted here for the *prevention* of crime :—

" *Boston, March* 6, 1845.

" It is just ten years since the Legislature granted an act of incorporation under the name of ' The Boston Asylum and Farm School for Indigent Boys.' Previous to that period there had been two corporations, whose plans had been somewhat different, yet whose objects were substantially the same. The ' Boston Asylum had been incorporated as early as 1814. Its general purpose was to relieve, instruct, and employ indigent boys belonging to the town of Boston, and the claims of orphans were to be particularly regarded. The plan of the ' Farm School' was proposed in 1832, and the Society was incorporated the year following. The object of this society was ' the education and reformation of boys, who, from loss of parents or other causes, were exposed to extraordinary temptations, and in danger of becoming vicious and dangerous or useless members of society.' In the summer of 1833, the Farm School was commenced on Thompson's island. In 1834, it was thought by the friends of both institutions that more good would be accomplished by a union of the two schools, that a larger number of exposed children could enjoy the advantages of proper physical and moral education at the school on Thompson's Island, than if the two institutions continued separate. The proposal to unite the two was fully agreed upon in May, 1834, and in March, 1835, the Legislature recognised the two institutions as one.

" There had been before this in our city, public penitentiaries established by municipal authority, but *this* was strictly a private corporation. To enter the former, (even the house of reformation for juvenile offenders) every child must be charged under oath in open court with some criminal act against the civil law, and for that act must be publicly tried, convicted, and sentenced. The Farm School was intended for indigent and exposed children, who had committed no crime, and who might be rescued from impending evil by timely care. Its object was to take the young from the midst of temptation, to shield them in their tender years, to give them proper mental and moral culture, and thus, without any stigma being attached to them, open for them a happy home, and return them to society fitted to become exemplary and useful citizens.

" From the establishment of this institution to the present time, it has been a source of extensive good. The children of intemperate and profligate parents have been taken from evil influences, and surrounded by many advantages. The sons of widows, whose parents with their small earnings could not do for their children as they would, have here found guardians and friends ; and orphans, who have been left without protectors or competent advisers, have been received within the walls of a Christian asylum, where they have listened to good counsel, and acquired habits of order, industry, and usefulness.

" Since the opening of the school in 1833, over four hundred boys have received the benefit of its instructions, and nearly all of them have now gone forth to take their part in the active duties of life.

" There has been but one death during the three last years, and 37 have been apprenticed by the institution, and placed under the charge of their friends. During the summer the boys have had the opportunity of frequent sea-bathing; and during the winter they have enjoyed warm baths. They are up at sunrise and retire at eight o'clock. Their food is simple and good. Their rooms are properly warmed and well ventilated, and all the pupils have much exercise in the open air. They enjoy innocent sports in the winter, and each boy has a flower-garden, the cultivation of which through the summer, is considered an agreeable amusement. One favorable result of this is a remarkable degree of health. For more than three years there has been no occasion to call a physician upon the Island on account of sickness. Any one visiting the institution would be impressed by the general appearance of vigor, the elasticity of frame, and the cheerfulness of countenance, which characterize the whole school.

" The boys are partly occupied upon the farm, and partly in the school, and also render assistance in the various domestic arrangements of the family. Many of them have become well versed in the practical skill of farming. During the summer the boys who are of sufficient age, work one week upon the farm, and pass the succeeding week in school. No exercise can be more healthy, and no labor can tend more than this to promote industrious habits, or to give to each individual an occupation which may make him useful through life.

" In connexion with the school and the farm, we may say, that the moral and spiritual condition of the pupils has neither been forgotten nor neglected. It has always been considered an imperative duty to do all that could be done for the religious instruction of all connected with the Institution. The children are regularly assembled for morning and evening prayers, and no opportunity is lost of appealing to their higher and better nature. By example and by precept, it is hoped and expected that a good influence will be exerted over all. We are aware that going through the stated forms of worship, will not of itself infuse spiritual life, nor establish sound principles. Still, if forms are connected with devout feeling in those who take in them a more prominent part, they may be the instruments of great good. And, if in addition to the mere form, there is a general spirit of excellence thrown over every duty, like an atmosphere, and flowing through every pleasure and privilege, as the very soul of its being, then we may hope that the young mind will through these be won to truth and virtue. Thus, in the singing of hymns, and in asking a blessing, and returning thanks, at each meal, there is an appropriateness and a power, which can hardly help exerting a salutary influence upon the youthful character ; an influence which will not be effaced in the days of its manhood. Upon each Sabbath there are religious services, which are adapted to the wants and condition of the pupils, and which they consider it a privilege to attend. On twenty-three Sundays of the past year, gentlemen from the city have addressed the children. There are now seventy boys under our care.

" There are many institutions in our commonwealth established for the *punishment* of crime, but this is for the far nobler purpose of *preventing* it.

The House of Refuge in the city of New York, appeared to me in all respects, one of the best regulated institutions of the kind I have seen. It admits of some changes for the better, and more thorough moral teaching of the inmates ; but, as it is, is of great usefulness ; it is a blessing to its inmates, and to society. The total of its inmates, the 1st of January, was 321. The boys were employed at making chair-frames, and seating them with cane ; in manufacturing paper cases, razor-strops, and pocket-books ; in making shoes, and mending them ; and in some household services. The girls are employed in washing, making and mending the apparel, and in all the departments of housewifery as practised here. The health of the establishment is remarkably good, notwithstanding the defective ventilation of the buildings. Remarkable cleanliness is preserved throughout the institution. Frequent bathing helps to maintain both mind and body in good condition. This universal truth, it is to be hoped, will become universal practice. As the periods of sentence expire, the boys are apprenticed to farmers chiefly ; but a few to sea-service and others to trades. The girls are chiefly apprenticed to household labor. Large numbers do well, and I have thought that most of those who are returned to the institution, if they had been more fortunately established with persons competent to train them, would have continued to conduct well.

The Farms, or the Farm-schools, on Long-Island, for the children removed from the city alms-house, New York, were purchased and occupied some years since, and usually contain from six to eight hundred children. Though many defects are apparent in the organization and administration of these departments for indigent boys and girls, many benefits have been secured by their establishment; and especially when we recollect from what conditions of wretchedness these poor children have been rescued, we are better able to appreciate the advantages they possess, and are less disposed to censure defects or complain of omissions. The establishments are to be removed from Long Island, to a more commodious situation, on Randall's island. I have been informed improvements are to be made in the modes of discipline and instruction, and facilities will be furnished for classifying the children, and placing them under a more judicious supervision. Mr. Coombe visited these Farm-schools in 1838, and his searching remarks deserve to be remembered, and repeated till the defects of which he wrote are remedied. I have myself felt when at the Farms their truth and justness. " The children sleep in an atmosphere, the consequences of which are visible. Many of them are suffering under opthalmia, and they generally present that sunken, inanimate, and unhappy aspect, which betokens blood in a bad condition, from *imperfect nutrition*, and *impure air*. There is no stinting of food, but the *digestive functions suffer from confinement in an unwholesome atmosphere*, and hence the nutrition is imperfect."

The House of Refuge in Philadelphia has been established since the 1st of December, 1828, and has received more than eighteen hundred inmates. The average age of those admitted in 1844 was, boys 14¼ years, girls 14 years. The ladies, twelve in number, who compose the visiting committee, for the girls' department, are some of them at the institution weekly, and report favorably of ' the order, neatness, economy, and good management, which pervade every part of it.' General good health prevails. The following extract from the report of the managers, presented to the legislature, January, 1845, will show the objects of the institution, and its discipline :—

" The great object of the Institution is the reformation of the young, who have left the paths of virtue.

" At the commencement and close of each day, the family join in prayer and thanksgiving to the Almighty ; and they attend the services of the chapel twice on the first day of the week. The Board acknowledge the kindness of ministers of different religious denominations, in giving their useful attendance at the House. The Sunday school for the boys is conducted by several of the Managers, assisted by some of their friends, and is in good order. That for the girls continues under the care of the same excellent lady, who has for several years, zealously and successfully superintended it. A number of books has been added to the Library.

" In the boys' school no change has been made ; the average time of tuition being about four hours a day. The Board have been enabled to add one hour a day to the instruction given to the girls. Arrangements have been made to introduce the manufacture of pocketbooks and razor-strops at the commencement of this year. This, with book-binding, caning seats for chairs, and manufacturing furniture for umbrellas, will afford constant, useful, and suitable employment for the male pupils. The females, in addition to school education, are taught tailoring, mantua-making, and the usual branches of housewifery. They also make and mend the clothing, and do the washing of the inmates. A new and convenient wash-house, with bathing rooms, has been erected for the girls.

" The Managers would not be understood to hold out the expectation that reformation can be accomplished in every case; but they are enabled to succeed in a large majority of cases.

" The Board would again urge upon parents and guardians, as well as upon magistrates, the importance of placing in the Refuge those who have just entered on a career of vice, and of not waiting until evil habits, by long indulgence, have become, in a great degree, fixed. Many children might be saved, if their vicious propensities were checked as soon as they began to develope themselves, who are now irretrievably ruined by the mistaken affection or culpable negligence of those who have the charge of them."

There is no House of Refuge for Juvenile Offenders in Maryland; but the Baltimore Manual Labor School, an institution for indigent boys, is worthy of notice, and of the liberal patronage of the citizens. I refer to this establishment with great pleasure, as the nucleus, around which we may hope to see gathered many excellent influences.

" In the month of December, 1840, the Directors having before obtained an act of Incorporation from the State, solicited subscriptions to enable them to carry out the benevolent object of the charter. A farm of 140 acres was purchased, on which were a stone dwelling and a large Barn with a Meat and Spring-house, about seven miles from the city. In March, the Farmer took possession of the farm; and on the 3d April, the first beneficiaries were received, the number of which had gradually increased to fifteen by the succeeding 21st July. Mr. J. J. Fogg, Teacher, entered upon his duties the 22d May. Although the farm-house was not more than sufficient to accommodate comfortably the Farmer with his family, he submitted to inconvenience, rather than reject, applicants, some of which were peculiarly destitute. In the course of the summer a frame-building was erected, which is capable of accommodating thirty boys as lodgers in the upper story, whilst in the lower one, it affords a school and eating rooms, with a washing apartment. This building was completed about the middle of October, and in the course of the succeeding six months, the full complement which the present buildings can accommodate, with a due regard to health and comfort, was made up. Of the thirty-four boys that now remain in the school, June, 1843, nine only could read in the simplest sentences at the time of their entrance, whilst the other twenty-five were ignorant of, or only knew the alphabet. Now, eighteen can read, write, and cypher, in a manner creditable to their teacher and themselves. Twelve can read well, are learning to write, and have been taught the four rules of mental arithmetic. The other four are beginning to read in simple sentences. Their unvaried health bears ample testimony to the salubrity of the farm, and their general deportment proves that their morals have not been neglected. It is provided by the charter, that each scholar who is able to read, shall be furnished with a Bible, and encouraged to read it at all proper seasons. It is also read by the Teacher, or one of the scholars, to all collectively as part of the regular morning and evening exercises ; and each boy, who is qualified, is required to read a chapter as the first of the morning duties, when assembled in the school room.

" The establishment proposes to imbue the young with a love of GOD and the love of man, and thus enable them to discharge that part which insures respectability and usefulness here, and ' in the world to come eternal life.' "

When I was last in Baltimore, July 1845, the operations of this school were temporarily suspended, on account of putting up new and more commodious buildings. These, when completed, will afford means for extended usefulness. The by-laws of the institution, defining the duties of the superintendent, teacher, and master, are judicious, and secure good discipline.

COUNTY JAILS, ETC.

Neither my leisure nor the limits assigned for this pamphlet will permit me to enter as fully upon this subject as I have designed, and the consideration of the poor-house system, and the condition of the poor-houses, I must defer altogether to a future time.

The six county prisons, of several hundred which I have visited and revisited in the Northern and Middle States, which most claim notice for their good discipline, are three on the silent system with labor, severally at South Boston, Mass. ; at Hartford, and at New-Haven, in Connecticut ; and three established on the separate system, severally at Philadelphia, Harrisburg, and West-Chester, in Pennsylvania. There are many other prisons, in the Northern and Middle States, which are well ordered *as mere detaining prisons,* but to which formidable exceptions must be made from the indiscriminate association of all classes of offenders, and who are also without employment either for the mind or the hands. These nurseries of vice claim early and efficient attention. Furnish them ever so well, keep them ever so clean, supply ever so sufficient, and well-prepared food, as at fifty or a hundred prisons I could indicate, but what does all avail, if the habits of daily life are becoming constantly more disastrous, and the soul is perishing for lack of the bread of life, and the waters of salvation ?

In a Memorial which was presented in my name to the Legislature of Pennsylvania, January, 1845, relating chiefly to the condition of the insane poor in alms-houses, and to convicts in the prisons committed in an insane condition, I have described three county prisons, which are established on the separate system, as follows :—

Dauphin County Jail at Harrisburg, is undoubtedly one of the best conducted county prisons in the United States. Like the Jail in Chester County it adopts the separate system with employment, and such instruction and advantages, as prisons constructed on this plan, secure to morals and habits. The provisions are excellent, and the food well prepared, and supplied in sufficient quantities. As a system, it is subject, in common with the Philadelphia and Chester county prisons, to the objection of retaining criminals whose offences render them subject to the State Penitentiaries, and to terms of imprisonment exceeding a year in duration. This mistake will, it is believed, be remedied both by justice, and a necessity which a little longer experience will make plain. The discipline and moral training of the Eastern and Western Penitentiaries, adapt them to effect the objects of prison detention for extended sentences more surely, than it is possible to secure in county prisons, where there are no teachers qualified and expressly appointed, to give appropriate instruction during the week.

Religious service is held in the Dauphin County Jail on every Sabbath afternoon, by the clergy of Harrisburg, who have volunteered their services, and so fulfil the law of Christ, preaching repentance and the forgiveness of sins, 'unto the poor and the prison-bound.' This instruction needs to be followed up by additional lessons. Many are profoundly ignorant upon the plainest principles of morals, so far as teaching and example have reached them. They need help in these things ; more aid than the inspectors or warden can have leisure to give. There is a well-chosen library. Repeated visits to this jail have satisfied me of the kind and just discipline which prevails. Punishments are infrequent, and when imposed, are of no greater severity or duration than is absolutely necessary for securing compliance with the mild and needful regulations of the institution.

The dimensions of the cells are 8 feet by 15, and 10 high ; lighted at one end near the ceiling. Pure water is introduced through iron pipes, and the cells are maintained warm and dry by means of hot water thrown through small iron pipes conveyed through each cell. The bunks are furnished with a straw bed, replaced as often as necessary ; and a sufficient quantity of clean bed-clothing. The apparel of the prisoners is comfortable, and adapted to the season. I have always found them in health and as good condition, physically, as the same number of persons following like employments and of steady habits abroad. On Jan. 1st, 1844, say the inspectors, in their report of the prison, there were *twenty-three* prisoners—fourteen of which were sentenced to labor ; four to imprisonment, ('who might have employment if they wished,') and five also, conditionally employed, were waiting trial. During the year 1844, there were received *one hundred and sixty-five* prisoners, and, during the same period, *one hundred and sixty-nine have been discharged ;* leaving in prison, January 1st, 1845, fourteen. *Died none.* The health of the prisoners is excellent.

The inspectors also remark, ' As to the efficacy of the system of separate confinement, *combined with labor,* being the most perfect yet devised for the punishment and reformation of offenders, our experience during the past year, fully confirms all that our remarks expressed in the last annual report—*giving precedence* to the ' Pennsylvania, or separate system.',

Chester County Jail, at West-Chester, (Penn.) is built of stone, upon the plan of separate imprisonment. The cells are of good size, perfectly clean, and well aired. The provisions supplied are of excellent quality. The allowance is three meals daily, and as much as satisfies the appetite. There has been but one death, by disease in four years, and this was by consumption, developed before admission ; and one prisoner was pardoned in consumption, who was also sick when received. One man, who was received in a state of intoxication, committed suicide. The warden reports to the board of inspectors, as follows :

We had in prison on the 1st of May, 1843,			....	32
We received, during the year, white males,			....	41
"	"	"	females,	3
Colored males,			....	25
" females,			....	4
Making in all,			....	105
In prison on the 1st of May, 1844,			....	28

" The total number sentenced to labor, during four years, since removing from the old prison, is 79. Of these, 47 could read and write ; 24 could not read nor write ; and 8 could read only. 33 of these prisoners were intemperate ; 28 of them temperate, and 18 were moderate drinkers."

I visited this prison in July, and saw all the prisoners, of which there were 29. 20 of these were convicts, and 9 were waiting trial. They were in excellent health, often replying to my inquiry in the words, ' I am right hearty.' They conversed cheerfully, were clean in their persons and apparel, and presented a remarkable contrast to the inmates of 68 prisons I have since visited.

Two of the prisoners above named, though in apparent health, were insane; the insanity of one was produced by irregular life and intemperance. The case of the other I did not learn. They both were in comfortable rooms, and were carefully attended. This prison is deficient in moral instruction. I saw a letter written by a prisoner, who had served out his time, and settled to an honest life. It was addressed to the warden, and shows that he was sensible of the kind influences which had been extended to him in prison :—

" Mr. Robert Irwin :—Sir :—I cannot but think, from the gentlemanly manner you treated me while I was with you, you would be glad to hear from me; and I do assure you, I shall always feel the most sincere gratitude and affection for you, and the other officers connected with the hall. The kind and manly course, pursued by you and all in authority, is calculated to reform any one that has the least spark of honesty left in his heart. I have, by sad experience, found that any, but an honest and upright course, will lead to wretchedness and misery."

The Philadelphia County Jail, at Philadelphia, situated in the district of Moyamensing, is a massive stone building, in the Gothic style of architecture. From the rear of the front edifice, the extensive halls run back at right angles; these contain three tiers of cells on either side. The two upper tiers are reached by means of railed corridors and galleries extending the entire length of the blocks which are ventilated and lighted from the roof. One block is appropriated to prisoners before trial. The other receives convicts who are sentenced, and who are here furnished with employment, and subject to a wholesome, but not rigid discipline. These blocks are exclusively for the male prisoners. The women's prison, divided by a high wall, and intervening garden, is a separate building and establishment, disconnected in all domestic arrangements from the men's prison. This department is especially well ordered, clean, comfortable, and well managed. The prisoners are supplied with suitable work—and with books; and have the benefit of moral and religious teaching, (not at the expense of the city or county,) from the moral instructor, and from an association of pious and devoted women, who spare no pains to reclaim the offenders, and restore the outcast. Their benevolent efforts are not confined to the prisoners during their terms of detention, but they endeavor to extend care and influence beyond the walls of the prison. Their disinterested and faithful exertions, sometimes meet with their highest reward, in the good results which attend upon and follow these labors. There are many in all prisons, who set at nought counsel and scorn reproof; but this is no argument whereby a Christian community would find justification in refraining from employing every consistent and reasonable exertion to recover the sin-sick soul—to inspire virtuous sentiments, to raise the fallen, and to strengthen the weak. The moral teacher, in this prison, is a missionary employed by a benevolent society. Would it be more than justice demands, since the courts sentence so many convicts to these prisons, for long terms, for the city to appoint and support a chaplain, at its own cost? The many hundred prisoners in the county jail, though a very unpromising class of pupils, certainly not the less on that account, should be faithfully visited and instructed.* Is it not a mistake, however, to sentence to the county prison, offenders, whose crimes make them legitimate subjects for the Eastern Penitentiary ? Sent there, where sufficient and effective arrangements are made for teaching the ignorant, and nourishing the moral nature ; where the regulations are, all in all, better adapted for their benefit, than can be those of the county prison ; they would be subject, not to a severer discipline, but would receive a stricter justice, whether we consider their rights as men, or their condemnation as criminals.

The cells of Moyamensing prison, are of good and convenient size, well lighted, tolerably ventilated, and in winter, well warmed. They are maintained clean, and well furnished, and are supplied with pure water, by pipes. The food is of good quality, and of sufficient quantity. It is well prepared, and usually distributed with care. I have visited all the cells in this extensive prison, and conversed with the prisoners, and, having spent the largest part of nine days in a diligent examination of their condition, and of the general arrangements and the discipline, I do not hesitate to say it is conducted in a manner highly creditable to the officers, whose duty it is to govern and direct its affairs. There are some defects, but they may be chiefly remedied with due attention. Well chosen additions to the library are much needed, as also care in the distribution of the books. The prisoners were at liberty to communicate to me their grievances, if they had any, and to represent their condition, without restraint. The only grave complaint, and it was twice repeated, was from a prisoner who desired a greater *variety* of food—mutton and veal to vary his meat diet, and a larger variety of vegetables! There were three or four insane men, who had been committed on various petty charges, and were not subjects for this prison nor any other.

The County-prison at Hartford, is constructed on the Auburn plan, and is under excellent discipline. The keeper is very much interested in promoting the best good of the prisoners,

* Judge Parsons, whose abilities as a jurist, and habits of critical investigation, entitle him to respect and confidence, says, " from my frequent visits to this institution, I am led to believe if there was one improvement in its discipline and arrangement, all the objects in punishment would be effected as well in this place, as in any other prison in the Commonwealth. There are at this time, September, 1843, *one hundred and eighty-six convicts*, in the prison, male and female, under sentence, in solitary confinement at labour. There are *three hundred and eighty-six other prisoners*, consisting of those sentenced for misdemeanors, vagrants, persons convicted for breaches of the peace, and those awaiting trial, making in all *five hundred and seventy two.* To render the organization of the Moyamensing prison complete, it is believed there ought to be a moral instructor, at the expense of the public who created this institution In my opinion, the object of those who achieved this great enterprise, will never be fully accomplished without it."

both physically and mentally ; the number of prisoners is small, there being but 32 cells, and these not often all occupied ; four of these, on the first floor are for punishment, and not therefore in daily use. The dimensions of the cells are too confined, being 10 feet by 5, and 7 high ; these are ventilated, and contain each an iron bedstead, with clean sacking and bed-clothing. The area on the left as you enter, is used as the work-shop, and is but 12 feet wide. Moral and religious instruction is more faithfully supplied here by *officers* and authorised visitors, than in any County Prison or House of Correction in New England. Though the plan of this prison has many excellences, it has also prominent defects which should be avoided in any prisons hereafter constructed.

The County prison at New-Haven, I found in good order, and so much better suited for the reformation of the prisoners, and a general control of them, than most prisons, that I feel no disposition to enter upon the apparent defects. The County prisons, at Norwich, (Conn.) and at Ipswich, (Mass.) I have not lately visited ; they are, in most respects, well reported of ; but it is said, there is a deficiency of moral and general instruction.

The county House of Correction at South Boston is well built, and is excellently planned for carrying out successfully the purposes of prison government, &c. In former years I often visited this prison ; latterly more rarely, on account of distant journeyings. I never found it other than in good order ; the law of the place, as of other city institutions within the stock-ade, being, apparently, that ' nothing is clean when it can be made cleaner.' The discipline is efficient, and as mild as the Auburn system of congregated labor will permit. The 3d of Sept. 1845, there were 225 prisoners, 74 of which were women, all sentenced by the municipal and police courts. Quite too many of the convicts are discharged by pardons and remission of sentence ; and too many prisoners escape imprisonment by the very injudicious imposition of fines, and the other equally injudicious acceptance of bail. There are 360 cells, which are perfectly clean, and admirably ventilated. The stoves for heating the lodging cells and areas in winter, are of better construction than any I have before seen in prisons.

The prisoners bathe in the salt-water, in a commodious bathing house, once a week during the mild seasons; and they bathe in warm water once a fortnight, throughout the cold months. The health of the place is remarkable, and the deaths few, considering the previous habits of the convicts. The women's work-rooms are well governed and arranged. The cells are suitably furnished. The hospital is faithfully attended, and entirely comfortable. The laundry, bakery, and cook rooms, are in most admirable order. The food is of good quality and well prepared.

The chaplain holds two services on Sunday. There is, at an early hour, a Sunday school for the women. The teachers are from the city, are much devoted to the improvement of the convicts, and extend a judicious care over all who, at the expiration of their sentences, give evidence of a disposition to lead an amended life. The library of this prison is not creditable to those whose duty it is to see the prisoners supplied with this means of improvement.

This prison, in all respects, ranks before the State prison at Charlestown; and, while it has an equally difficult class of prisoners to discipline and reform, sustains discipline, without the use of the lash, and with fewer punishments in proportion to the actual number of transgressions. The product of convict labor has never supported this prison, though its financial concerns have always been well managed.

More detailed annual reports of the prison would be desirable and very useful. This House of Correction takes precedence of all penitentiaries in the Northern States, not excepting even that of Connecticut.

I cannot conclude these remarks without renewedly urging the remoddelling of, and the reformation of the county jails in the United States. It is infinitely worse to arrest offenders, and lodge them in jails where safe custody is the only consideration to which weight is attached, than to leave them at large. It is worse for offenders, and worse ultimately for society. In the first instance, they inevitably become more corrupt. They have no escape, if they wish it, from vicious companionship; and, when it is farther recollected, that these prisoners include the really guilty, the merely suspected, and these of both sexes, and all ages, we cannot fail to see what is the imperative duty of the citizens of every county throughout the Union, in which this subject has not received so much deliberation and action as to have procured a remedy for neglects and abuses, worthy only of an age when vice was openly countenanced, and crime was at a premium. Hundreds certainly, more probably thousands, have for some first and trivial offence, been lodged in county-prisons, exposed to the impure and contaminating influences of indiscriminate companionship. Here they have become hardened, here lost all self-respect, and have yielded day by day, to the mind-poisoning, moral miasm of these legalized receptacles.

From these great evils, society only can redeem the offender. If the offence is slight, or if suspicion alone attaches to the prisoner, there being no question of the justice of detention, the wrong is resolved into the injustice of compelling bad companionship, and making a jail a county free-school of vice. If the prisoner be already confirmed in vicious propensities and an evil life, it is manifestly very bad policy, all other considerations aside, to make him the teacher of what is mischievous and destructive of public safety, to those not confirmed in the practice of vicious excesses and criminal misdeeds. I have heard the observation that persons do not reach the jail till they are far on in paths of wickedness; this is a misapprehension, resulting from want of correct information. I could adduce a very large number of examples to the contrary, especially of *young* persons and *children*. As such may be gathered in every county-town in the Union, not recently incorporated, it is quite unnecessary to enter upon details here.

Let all prisons hereafter be constructed so as at least to admit classification; if not in a greater measure of entire separation. This was secured in most of the old prisons to some extent; but in several new prisons on the Auburn plan, as at Lowell, Rochester, Buffalo, &c. &c., these evils are greatly increased in the new jails. I refer all interested in these subjects to the prisons, and the officers of the prisons, for confirmation of these facts. Even at the new prison at Springfield, where employment is given and required for the men, defects will be found quite beyond the control of the officers to remedy. I did not learn what disposition was made of the prisoners on Sundays; but, if shut into their very narrow, low cells, which have no ventilation, although the prison is neatly kept, I think the punishment too severe for prisoners, whether waiting trial or convicted, and a discipline not calculated to improve or amend either.

Early in March, 1843, a comprehensive, and excellently devised document, relating to the regulation and improvement of County-jails in Ohio, was laid before the legislature, and passed into an act, ordaining wholesome supervision and reforms in the county jails. It is much to be regretted that this act has not been more effectually and precisely enforced. From all I have seen and been able to ascertain, I should judge that the jail at Columbus most nearly fulfils the requirements of this law, and perhaps none fails to a greater extent in all the requirements of the act, than the county prison at Zanesville. Several county prisons, constructed on the Auburn plan, in Ohio, New York, and Massachusetts, do not, in my opinion, or in that of their officers with whom I have conversed, correct the abuses of the old prisons, but, in some respects, decidedly increase them; as at Chilicothe and Cincinnati, Ohio, (the last named is described to me by friends resident there;) the jails at Rochester and Buffalo, in New York, which I have repeatedly visited; the new jail at Springfield, Mass. which has no ventilation in the cells, and other defects not important to specify; the jail at Lowell, and the prison at East Cambridge, (Mass.) Others might be specified, if it were any object to increase the list. Several prisons, constructed for the adoption of the separate system, with employment, as yet have not commenced the much needed reform of their discipline: as the jail in Pittsburg, (Penn.) and the jails at Newark and Patterson, New Jersey. A new prison has been built near Jersey City, but it is deficient in the most important modern improvements, and is a very bad specimen of prison architecture, affording no sufficient means for preserving cleanliness, for heating, supplying with water, or of suitable ventilation. Employment is not provided for.

The Halls of Justice(!) more familiarly known as "The

Tombs," in the city of New York, imperatively demand a speedy and thorough reorganization and reform. As receiving prisons, they are a disgrace to the civilized and Christian community which instituted them; and as schools of the most shocking and demoralizing influences, I am sure none more debasing and unholy can be designated, and if these facts were not notorious, I should not pause here upon assertions.

APPENDIX.

WOMEN CONVICTS—Very few, usually no women-convicts, are found in the State prisons in Maine, New-Hampshire, and Vermont. In Massachusetts these are not committed to the State prison, but are sent to the Houses of Correction, severally in Middlesex, Essex, and Suffolk counties; in the other counties they are sometimes detained in the jails. In each of the local prisons above named, matrons govern the women's department. In Connecticut prison there are 20 women under the supervision of an excellent matron. Unfortunately the present discipline of this prison affords for the women no period but Sundays for instruction, except in mechanical labors. In New-York all the women state convicts are sent to a prison at Sing Sing; these average about 72, and are under the direction of a matron, who, with her assistants, are much interested in the improvement of those under their charge. New-Jersey prison has but two women-convicts, and no matron. The Eastern Penitentiary has 20 women-convicts. This department I have often visited, and always found in order; neatness and good behaviour appear to be the rule and practice of the prison; the exceptions being very rare. The matron is vigilant, and fills her station in a manner to secure respect and confidence. The women are chiefly employed in making and repairing apparel, and have full time for the use of books, and the lessons which are assigned weekly by the ladies who visit the prison to give instruction. In the Eastern District, a portion of the women-convicts, since the building of the Philadelphia, Chester, and Dauphin county prisons, have been sentenced to these, where they come under similar discipline. In the Moyamensing prison they possess corresponding moral advantages and means of receiving instruction, as those who are sent to the State prison. In the Western Penitentiary are 7 women-convicts, no matron; in Ohio prison are 6 women-convicts, no matron ; in Virginia prison are 15 women-convicts, no matron ; in the Washington prison, D. C., 4 women, a year since, no matron ; in the Maryland prison were 15 women under the charge of an energetic matron, who earnestly desires to maintain order, without resorting to severe restraints and punishments ; these cannot be always dispensed with. There is too little provision for moral instruction in this department.

The product of women's labor in the State prisons, fails to meet the expenses of their department. I should judge it greatly more advantageous in all respects, to sentence women-convicts to the county houses of correction, rather than connect their prisons, with those of the men-convicts, especially also if their numbers are so few that it is judged inexpedient to appoint a matron.

NOTE.

See page 30.

There seems to have been an error of the press in the official document from which was quoted the average of pardons in the State of New-York, from the year 1825 to 1835 inclusive. The number stated, as 1 to 4, pardoned during those years, appears to be erroneous. I have not had the opportunity of consulting the *original* papers from which the document was printed.